WOMAN
EVOLVE

WOMAN EVOLVE

BREAK UP WITH YOUR FEARS
&
REVOLUTIONIZE YOUR LIFE

SARAH JAKES ROBERTS

W Publishing Group

An Imprint of Thomas Nelson

Published in Nashville, Tennessee, by W Publishing Group, an imprint of Thomas Nelson.

Thomas Nelson titles may be purchased in bulk for educational, business, fundraising, or sales promotional use. For information, please email SpecialMarkets@ThomasNelson.com.

Unless otherwise noted, Scripture quotations are taken from the New King James Version®. © 1982 by Thomas Nelson. Used by permission. All rights reserved.

Scripture quotations marked NIV are from the Holy Bible, New International Version®, NIV®. © 1973, 1978, 1984, 2011 by Biblica, Inc.® Used by permission of Zondervan. All rights reserved worldwide.

Any internet addresses, phone numbers, or company or product information printed in this book are offered as a resource and are not intended in any way to be or to imply an endorsement by Thomas Nelson, nor does Thomas Nelson vouch for the existence, content, or services of these sites, phone numbers, companies, or products beyond the life of this book.

Library of Congress Cataloging-in-Publication Data

Names: Roberts, Sarah Jakes, 1988– author.
Title: Woman evolve / Sarah Jakes Roberts.
Description: Nashville, Tennessee : W Publishing Group, an imprint of Thomas Nelson, [2021] | Includes bibliographical references. | Summary: "Reimagining the story of Eve, Sarah Jakes Roberts draws lessons from Scripture and from her own life that show women how to use the mistakes of their past to overcome the challenges of today. *Woman Evolve* teaches women that they can use failures and mistakes to break through to their future. Like Eve, they do not need to live defined by the past. Pastor Sarah says, 'Bruised heels can still crush serpents' heads.'"— Provided by publisher.
Identifiers: LCCN 2020045489 (print) | LCCN 2020045490 (ebook) |
    ISBN 9780785235545 (hc) | ISBN 9780785235569 (ebook) | ISBN 9780785235583 (IE)
Subjects: LCSH: Eve (Biblical figure) | Women—Religious aspects—Christianity. | Christian women—Religious life.
Classification: LCC BS580.E85 R63 2021 (print) | LCC BS580.E85 (ebook) |
    DDC 222/.11092—dc23
LC record available at https://lccn.loc.gov/2020045489
LC ebook record available at https://lccn.loc.gov/2020045490

Printed in the United States of America

21 22 23 24 25 LSC 10 9 8 7 6 5 4 3 2 1

*To every woman determined to abandon what was and
bold enough to discover what could still become . . .
this one is for us.*

CONTENTS

ONE

RESCUE EVE

Then God blessed them, and God said to them, "Be fruitful and multiply; fill the earth and subdue it; have dominion over the fish of the sea, over the birds of the air, and over every living thing that moves on the earth."

—GENESIS 1:28

Three years ago I fell deeply in love with Eve. Yes, the Garden of Eden Eve, the woman who basically ruined God's plan for humanity over a piece of fruit.

I know what you're thinking: *Fall in love with Eve? How is that even possible? The woman most popularly known for being the gateway of sin, debauchery, cramps, bloating, labor pain, dysfunctional relationships, insecurities, depression, disease, stretch marks, acne . . . ?* Yes. That's the one.

For years I rolled my eyes whenever Eve's name came up. I saw her as the woman who had *one* job and failed so miserably that it changed my life, and yours, thousands upon thousands of years later. Before it could even begin. A fantasy of traipsing around a tropical garden with a flat tummy, picking organic fruit from trees—never worrying about the cost of living, global warming, or obsessing over social media—comes to a screeching halt over a little ol' piece of fruit. Picked from a forbidden tree.

I've always had *big* plans to get to heaven and give Eve a full neck-twisting, eye-rolling, hand-clapping dissertation on the effects her choice has had on the rest of us. But all of that changed at a women's conference. I noticed that all the volunteers (and most of the registrants) wore matching shirts. This isn't uncommon at a women's event; however, these shirts were different. They displayed the names of women in the Bible who are celebrated for their commitment and faith: "Sarah. Ruth. Esther. Mary. #squadgoals."

Since we are just getting to know each other, now may be a good time to tell you something you should probably know about me. From time to time, there's this petty part of my brain that needs to be reminded that I know Jesus. Is that anybody else's testimony?

That day at the conference, that petty part of my brain tapped me on my proverbial shoulder and whispered, "Chiiillle, look! You ain't the only one who doesn't want Eve on her squad." I immediately smiled at the thought.

As I walked from the backstage holding room into the crowded auditorium, I looked over the audience. The "Sarah. Ruth. Esther. Mary. #squadgoals" shirt was literally everywhere I turned. The band had taken their places on the stage. The singers had grabbed their microphones. The music was blaring, and everyone in the room was lifting their voices in worship. But I was stuck.

I couldn't shake the feeling that something was wrong. I should have been opening my heart and lifting my hands to sing along with all the others. After all, in just a few short moments I was scheduled to take the platform and share a message meant to confront, transform, and empower the women in the room to pursue the vision God had when He created them. Yet all I could think about was Eve.

Logically I knew why her name was not on the shirts. Seriously. Who in their right mind wants Eve on their squad? She was so easily tempted and manipulated to abandon what she knew was right and engage with what would leave her (and the rest of us) in the world struggling.

If an actual lightbulb appeared over our heads each time we had an epiphany, in that moment a high-megawatt beam would've been shining brilliantly over mine!

Compassion for Eve hit me like a ton of bricks. This time I wasn't viewing her from my high horse but from a position of empathy that can only come from knowing what it's like to be in someone else's shoes. There I was, in the middle of a women's conference, where the virtues of women who showed ridiculous faith and righteousness were being proclaimed, but all I could think about was Eve—my heart longing to go back to the garden to tell her that she still had value, promise, and worth.

YOU'VE GOT SOME EVE IN YOU

Value. Promise. Worth. Aren't those the words we all need to hear? Especially when we find ourselves in our own inevitable *Eve* moments? Haven't we all had a moment when we knew better but didn't do better?

Let's be honest. Our inclination to choose a path that pushes us further away from our moral, ethical, spiritual, financial, physical, relational, or emotional goals is not a foreign concept. Yet Eve has been vilified for making a similar choice. One we all can relate to making at some point, in some way.

If you raised your eyebrow at that last sentence, allow me a moment to prove it to you.

Every day we are given many opportunities to choose what we know is good and right for us. But if you're like me, there are times throughout the day when my discipline to do what I know is good and right is overshadowed by the temptation to do what I know will ultimately slow my progress. In other words, you know what it's like to know better but not do better.

Maybe you're like me, and you "closet eat" french fries in the car before you get home with everyone's dinner. Or you overindulge and buy things you know you don't need (but convince yourself you really do). No doubt we all stalk the social media pages of those who have hurt us, allowing our thoughts of shame, anger, fear, anxiety, insecurity, and doubt to take the mic—sometimes to the point we no longer have the faith required to live life with integrity or confidence.

In those moments, when we choose to resist what we know we should do, we are subconsciously also choosing to live inwardly unfulfilled, envious, and apprehensive, in toxic relationships, and addicted, stressed, depressed, ashamed of ourselves . . . the list goes on and on, but all of it ends in a state of devastation. The truth is that no matter how easy people may make it seem, it can be incredibly challenging to abandon toxic habits and instead choose to do what we know is right.

This is by no means a judgment. If you're still on this planet, then there's an area of your life that is still growing to its maximum potential.

If you're journaling or taking notes—and if not, now is a good time to grab pen and paper; you're going to need it—I invite you to take a moment to look within your soul. What's an area of your life where you continue to repeat a cycle that ends with you feeling less valuable? That, my dear, is your forbidden fruit. Now, consider how evolving for the better in that area would change your life. That's the new pattern I want you to achieve. And to help you with these kinds of deeper reflections, I've added "Working It Out" opportunities in the chapters that follow. Please take a moment to pray each time before you begin to work it out. I think you'll be amazed at the way God honors those prayers and your work.

I'VE GOT SOME EVE IN ME

My first devastating foray with forbidden fruit was different from Eve's. I wasn't in a garden God created for my personal enjoyment and dwelling. I wasn't walking around in my birthday suit in the middle of the day, with grass mingling with my toes or birds chirping in the air. I can't even say there was a slithering serpent that got in my head and ruined my life.

The truth is there was no one to blame for the toxic pattern that infected my soul with fear, anxiety, and depression. I was very much complicit in the experiences that attempted to destroy my worth and value. Like Eve, I knowingly ate from a tree I knew would end in misery.

Ever since that wake-up moment on the conference stage, I've had one mission: rescue Eve and all the other women like her. Women like me. Women who are sometimes lost in a world that feels bigger than they are. Women who are attempting to recover after a setback. Women who want to bring forth good fruit despite the forbidden fruit they were exposed to. I want to serve them by helping them grow from wherever they are willing to start to the place God has marked as their finish line.

My purpose is to create environments where women feel safe enough to retrace their steps so they can see where pain, disappointment, or failure buried their hope, potential, and faith. Because when we dare to retrace our steps, we learn that those difficult experiences did not only hurt us. They changed the way we show up and engage in relationships, friendships, business, family, and the world in general.

Just because you've survived something doesn't mean you didn't experience damage. There is truly nothing more necessary for our journey of healing than acknowledging we've been damaged. How else can we heal unless we admit we're wounded?

For those of us who have found safety in not admitting, not digging into what was, let me offer some assurances. I'm not asking you to experience the heartbreak again. I'm not leading you into a cave. I'm not going to leave you stuck. We're finally going to lean in instead of running away. We're going to pass through a tunnel that allows us to reconnect with our soul, hopes, passion, and power. We're going to stop pretending that it never happened because there is a realization more powerful than any painful truth you've experienced. When you commit to growth after trauma, there is resurrecting power that demands your hope, potential, and faith to rise up. An even better version of you is waiting to emerge!

THE RESCUE

There is a well in you. That well has perspectives, disciplines, strategy, creativity, and paradigms that will consistently reveal to you what God knows about you in every season of your life. That well cannot be damaged. That well has not run dry. It's still tucked away in the corridor of your heart, and it's been waiting for a moment to spring forth. It will water the seeds of the woman God created you to become. No matter how much you have accomplished or how far you are from even getting started, if you're still alive, there is an even more powerful, purposeful woman waiting to take root and produce fruit within you. My job is to help you dig until that well springs up, and that version of you has no choice but to come forth.

That version of you is powerful because of her vulnerability and authenticity. She doesn't talk herself out of getting the support she needs to be free. That version of you is not ashamed of the path that has led her to where she is today. That version of you believes health is wealth, starts the business, goes back to school. That version of you spends and saves with financial stability (and overflow!) in mind. She shatters glass ceilings. That version of you is so whole that a relationship is the cherry on top, not a necessity. That version of you believes that her potential is limitless, and the sky is only another level—not a limit. She is empowered to continuously evolve because she's fascinated by how God will reveal His perfect plan and strength through her heart and hands. That version of you does not subscribe to the notion that this is exclusively a man's world, but *every* industry has room for a woman who is confident that she belongs wherever God sends her.

Our world was not given to just one gender to subdue. Genesis 1:28 says, "Then God blessed *them*, and God said to *them*, 'Be fruitful and multiply; fill the earth and subdue it; have dominion over the fish of the sea, over the birds of the air, and over every living thing that moves on the earth'" (emphasis added). That declaration was God's original intention for *all* of humanity. So, girl, this world literally needs you. We need you to be fruitful and multiply, not just with beautiful babies but with incredible ideas and opportunities. And if you don't commit to filling this earth, the alternative does

7

Subdue to overcome

not exclusively affect just you. The world is so interconnected that your empty spot gives permission for someone else to leave her spot unfulfilled too. Because when you subdue your giant, you teach the rest of us how to take ours down too.

Eve eating from the fruit did not change God's intention—it only changed how He would fulfill that intention. God still desired to partner with Adam, Eve, and all of humanity to unleash our ability to manifest His divinity on Earth. But because of her choice, Eve would have to take on the daunting task of seeing beyond the depravity of her present life to partner with God for her future.

moral corruption, wickedness

Every woman will have to fight Eve's fight to manifest God's vision of filling and subduing the earth. Eve had to fight to see where she fit in the world. She had to fight to look past her mistakes and to stay connected to God and others. Eve had to fight like the world depended on it—because it did. Imagine if we stopped minimizing our fight and recognized that no matter how small or minuscule it may seem, if it's keeping us from being better, it's a threat to not just us—it's a threat to the world.

It's not just low self-esteem. It's not just a little anxiety or depression. It's not just bitterness. It's a threat to who you are called to be on this earth. When you do not become better, the world cannot become better either.

Eve made a mistake, but she had proper perspective on how important it was to course correct. I've been on a mission to rescue Eve because she's been penalized for what she did but not recognized for how she showed up to fight back.

I no longer see Eve as the woman I vilified. I see her as a reflection of me and so many other women who've been able to see their futures only through a filter that fear, shame, and disappointment can create. I never felt passionate about starting a community for women to connect, grow, and inspire one another until I had this epiphany about Eve.

I wanted to shout from the rooftop that a woman who is determined to abandon what was must commit to the vulnerable process of evolving. It's impossible to maximize the potential that God has placed in each of us and stay the same. When we make room for transformation in our lives, we embody the definition of evolving. *Evolve* means to develop gradually, especially from a simple to a more complex form.

Now, listen, I know that life is already complex enough and simple sounds appealing, but to be complex is not the same as being complicated. *Complex* simply means consisting of many different and connected parts. There are so many different parts of who you are, but are they all connected? The creation story reveals that God doesn't create anything simple. Genesis 1:1 says He "created the heavens and the earth." It sounds simple, but one semester with astronomy as an elective will prove that there is nothing simple about the heavens.

Just as true as this is for the sky, it's true for you. There is so much more to you than the simplified perspective you have on your existence. You are a beautiful, vast, ornate demonstration of God's thoughts and hope for humanity. Eve had to learn this the hard way, and so did I. The pursuit of God's thoughts toward me, and every woman, birthed a desire for me to create community for women. Through our podcasts, events, social media, and curriculum, we're able to connect, support, challenge, and inspire one another to discover the best version of ourselves. I call it Woman Evolve, and the content of this book is inspired by the breakthroughs we've had together.

Notice how saying *evolve* very slowly you hear *Eve*. That's how much my revelation of her experience inspired me.

———

As my slight stalker obsession with Eve began to fully blossom, I felt deeply in my heart that the only way to begin the journey of saving every woman was to start with rescuing the first woman. I needed to go back in time and imagine being her and not just looking at her choices from the outside in. I needed to rescue her from who I thought she was. This journey felt so appropriate because in my own life I realized that my healing began the moment I wanted to rescue myself from who I was not so that I could discover who I could become.

I read through Genesis armed with my new compassion for Eve. Instantly I recognized more than her guilt. I saw her innocence. I recognized her strength. I realized how much courage she exhibited when she chose to be an active participant in her restoration process. I learned that she was not just the woman who ate from the forbidden fruit; she was the woman who paved a way for the ultimate Redeemer who would offer salvation to all humanity.

Throughout our time together in this book, I share what I've learned, and what I'm continuing to learn, about unearthing the gifts, talents, discipline, and stability that produce perpetual inner victory. Many women have influenced my development, certainly too many for me to list in this book. I feel, however, that it is important for me to introduce you to one of them in the way that I've come to know her.

Come with me, for a moment, back to the Garden of Eden.

MY FRIEND EVE

It was the way her eyes moved before her eyelids ever parted that indicated she was ready to be introduced to a whole new world. Flutter, shut, flutter, shut, she practiced the opening and closing of them until she finally allowed them to remain open. Then, slowly, she lifted her delicate hands to eye level. Like a newborn baby trapped in a woman's body, she stood in the middle of the garden, fascinated by her fingertips. The warmth from the sun covered every inch of her like a blanket. She studied the backside of her hands and marveled at the hints of red and gold peeking from beneath the top layer of her bronzed skin. Turning her hands over, she discovered the intersecting lines embedded on her palms. Her fingertips traced the trail of lines as they mingled and danced, creating abstract art unique to her tale. Her eyes roamed the length of her arms. Her right hand grazed the roundness of her left shoulder and the fragile protrusion of her collarbone. She paused only to rest the pads of her fingers in the cove that held her pulse. She took a moment and felt the rhythm of her blood flowing through her body—steady and controlled.

Slowly but surely, her focus drifted, and she began surveying the rest of her frame. Devoid of another woman's body to serve as a point of reference, she felt no need to compare the roundness of her tummy with others she'd seen. Nor could she judge the appropriate thickness of her thighs or ideal width of her hips. Instead, she did what so many of us fail to accomplish: she reveled in the beauty and simplicity of her existence. The woman was fascinated by the dimensions of her power. She had the innate ability to touch with a delicate finesse or with a firmness that demanded the recognition of her strength.

Still utterly consumed with her personal examination

of the body she now possessed, the woman's trance was suddenly broken when she heard the rustling of life happening around her. She took what she thought would be a quick glance around, but her eyes widened with astonishment and admiration as she surrendered to the beauty of her new home. The birds swirled above her head. The lush grass danced with her toes. The bushes crunched as the creatures passing by divided their square form. Undeterred by her stares, the creatures went about their way, not nearly as intrigued by her as she was by them. The rivers streamed with a familiar pulsating rhythm, reminding her of the beat she felt happening in the cove of her neck just moments before. The woman had so much to learn yet no urgency to do it. This moment, her introduction to the world, had to be fully breathed in.

She continued to skim the new land until the only being powerful enough to break her trance came into focus. In a world full of so many textures, colors, shapes, and forms, he was the only thing she'd seen thus far that resembled her own frame. The differences were subtle but undeniable. His shoulders were broader and arms much longer than her own. There was a bulge in his neck that resembled the fruit she'd observed on one of the trees. His face was decorated with hair that began by his ears and circled around his mouth. Her eyes landed on the corner of his lips and she noticed how they curved slightly upward. Instantly, she mirrored his expression. When she finally focused on his eyes, she had a knowing that while she stood taking in her environment, he'd been studying her.

He was standing there staring at her as if she were the

most fascinating organism he'd ever encountered. He surveyed every inch of her beauty with his eyes and became irrefutably mesmerized. It was the way their eyes locked that made the earth stand still. The flowers stopped their sway, and the breeze broke its pattern. It was almost as if the whole world were applauding that he'd finally found something akin to him.

He took her hand in his. Palm to palm their hands conveyed what their spirits already knew. Their connection began long before their fingers, presently intertwined, ever touched. It began in a realm much more divine. A realm that not even words could define. Immediately it became obvious that the sun would rise and set many times over before their infatuation with each other's presence grew dull.

He navigated their world with ease and comfort. She studied her environment like a new student eager to please and desiring to do well. He shared with her the names of all the creatures and plants. He exemplified the power they both possessed to command the earth to do as they wished. The man often stressed that everything was made in sequence of importance, with her entrance serving as the apex of all creation. It felt like the woman was late to a party that had been going on for hours. Her delayed entrance into the world meant she would have to catch up from last place while somehow exhibiting a confidence that relayed she deserved to be first. He tried to help by reminding her of the commandment that they'd been given when God handed them the "reins." God had said, "Be fruitful and multiply; fill the earth and subdue it; have dominion over the fish of the sea, over the birds of the air, and over every living thing that moves on the earth." This intimidating world was created to adjust to the tone she set, but she would have to be intentional about setting that tone or she would get lost in the rhythm the world set.

WHAT ABOUT US?

Can you imagine coming into the world as an adult woman? Everyone and everything has its place except you. You're simply still trying to understand if, and where, you fit.

The woman we know as Eve was pulled from the rib of the man and placed in an organized world where everything had a label, role, and united function. She was told to subdue the earth, but how can one subdue the unknown? She was charged with controlling a world that she did not even understand. No wonder all it took was one thought to change her tenor and undermine their success.

Eve's ability to succeed depended on how well she navigated and transformed the culture that predated her existence. Unfortunately, before she could begin producing from the safety of her new normal, one encounter changed everything forever. I wish I could say that this woman, my friend, had no control over how her story detoured, but that would not be entirely true. I don't believe it was her intention for things to veer as drastically as they did; however, I cannot deny that she knew before she gave in that trouble would begin.

Simply put, she knew better but didn't do better, but haven't we all been there? Should she be penalized forever for what she failed to do in that moment? Choose your answer wisely, because however you handle Eve's transgression will undoubtedly be how you handle the transgressions of others, especially your own.

If this were a courtroom, now would be the moment when I dramatically turn to the judge and say, "I rest my case." Because who can't relate to being fragile, ignorant, and susceptible to mental, emotional, and spiritual traps that ultimately change our mind and then our actions? I know quite a few women who can relate. In fact, I'm one of them.

And to think this all began when she was exploring her new world away from the man who served as her guide. He'd given her the rules and outlined the plan; he could have never imagined that a creature so crafty could have undermined their mission. In theory he was correct. The woman did not just obey a random command. She engaged in a conversation that changed her mind first, then her diet, and eventually her actions.

All it took was one question. One question invaded her mind, opened the floodgates, and changed her path: "Has God indeed said, 'You shall not eat of every tree of the garden'?" (Genesis 3:1). That's all it took to suck her into questioning herself and the power, purpose, and potential God granted her.

Narrowing down to a moment what happened in the garden when a woman sunk her teeth into a piece of fruit is far too easy. Closer examination reveals the trouble began long before she picked the fruit.

The moment the woman's truth was uprooted and replaced with inquisition is the moment humanity took a sharp turn.

Can you remember the first time your truth was uprooted? Can you remember the first time you no longer felt safe? Loved? Wanted? Liked? Good enough? Beautiful? Innocent? Can you remember how it made you question yourself and others? The serpent in the garden wasn't after Eve's appetite. He was after what she trusted as God's vision for her life. God's power in her life began to dissolve the moment she started questioning God's plan for her life.

For the longest time, I thought my trauma began when I became pregnant as a teenager. I know now that my pregnancy was just the moment I ate from the fruit. The seed of trauma began as a question, and the search for the answer is what led to my pregnancy and to every other issue that destabilized my world. That question, and so many other questions produced from it, would haunt me for many years before I finally discovered the only answer that mattered.

In full transparency, the question has not fully gone away, but the search for the answer has ceased. The question that started it all was "Do you really belong here?" The "here" changed over the years. Sometimes the "here" was family, other times it was school, occasionally it was relationships, and eventually it found its way into my career and purpose.

What question haunts you? What is it that finds a way to creep into the most unsuspecting moments of your life? That question is a seed that if not properly addressed will continue to control your actions.

You may want to change your thinking and actions. Perhaps you've wanted to change them for quite some time, but to no avail. When Eve was in the garden, engaging with the serpent, it was the question that ultimately changed her actions. Perhaps we should spend less time focusing on the action and more time discovering the root question that produced the action.

If we can get to the root, we can change the fruit.

TWO

KNOW BETTER

Now the serpent was more cunning than any beast of the field which the LORD God had made. And he said to the woman, "Has God indeed said, 'You shall not eat of every tree of the garden'?"

—GENESIS 3:1

My husband, Touré, and I live in Los Angeles. He's lived here most of his life. I've only been here six years.

Touré's status as a longtime resident of LA has granted him unprecedented knowledge of back roads and shortcuts that he uses to avoid the horrendous traffic. In fact, he knows six or seven ways to get across town. On the other hand, I know how to use the navigation app on my phone.

I can't begin to tell you how many minutes I have been stuck in traffic while Touré awaited my arrival. I look in the distance and see the unpredictable sea of red lights and my stomach drops. I watch the arm on my speedometer slowly lose momentum until I'm at a complete standstill. Stopped and frustrated, I immediately pull out my phone and consult the Waze app to see how delayed I will actually be.

If being late is hereditary, then I'm certain it was passed down to me from my mother, and, well, God is still working on me in this area. Nine times out of ten I leave the house with just enough time to arrive (but not enough time to park, let alone walk in). With intentional driving—not to be confused with speeding—and Waze, I can almost ensure that I'm close to on time but not embarrassingly late.

Given my husband's knowledge of the city, I make it a rule to give him a quick call before blindly obeying Waze. When I tell him my plan to use Waze, he asks me to screenshot the route Waze is taking me. Without fail, his phone has barely chimed in receipt of the screenshot when I hear his exasperated voice declaring, "No, no, no! Waze doesn't know what it's talking about. I'm *from* this city. Hop off on the next exit, make a left on Ventura, and head north on Sepulveda. When you get to Burbank, head east. Then hop back on the 101, and you should know your way from there."

———

You know what Waze is doing while my husband is defaming its notoriety? Homegirl is speaking to me in the calmest English accent. (I made my Waze fancy.) She is patiently waiting for me to make one simple turn. She's not inducing anxiety by trying to give me all the directions at once. She is also obviously aware that I'm directionally challenged, so there are no intimidating words, like *north*, *south*, *east*, or *west*.

Now I'm stressed. Waze is waiting for me, but my husband, who is well versed in the city, is insisting he knows a better route. Internally, I'm weighing my options. Do I take my husband's directions, or do I tell him that I'm stressed and would rather spend some time with my homegirl Waze? I've only got a split second to make a decision before I miss the opportunity to exit and come to another screeching halt in the blessed LA traffic. The pressure is mounting, and the clock is ticking. I have two competing routes ahead of me, with the added element that failure to make a decision will undoubtedly result in me being stuck. And late.

I wish choosing between Waze or Touré's routes was the most difficult dilemma in my life. I frequently find myself standing at challenging crossroads questioning which path to take.

WE HAVE A CHOICE

Have you been there? Life's crossroads are a bit more complicated than choosing what to do in traffic. Too often they feel like gambling. And, heaven forbid, if you've ever experienced the trauma of miscalculating a risk, it's even more challenging to finalize your decisions. I think we can all agree that it would be exponentially easier to quit a job if we knew that leaving would result in a successful career. And choosing vulnerability would be a no-brainer if we were assured it would not end in hurt.

As frustrating as it might be to have to choose between two traffic routes in a crossroads moment, that decision pales in comparison to navigating the multilane highway that is my mind. Chiiillle, that's an actual struggle! At least when I'm in LA traffic I know my destination. I have an approximate idea of how long it will take me to get there and how much fuel the trip will require.

When I'm at one of life's crossroads, I'm tasked with making a decision with almost no information. I'm expected to make a decision that will lead me to an unspecified location through an unfamiliar place. I never have any idea how much time, rest, hope, energy, or faith I'll need to get there.

This is the moment my anxiety buckles up in the back seat and begins making unnecessary commentary: *You should have never started this journey to begin with. You know if you fail it's going to prove what everyone has been thinking about you.* Did I mention my past is hog-tied in the trunk, demanding to know if we've arrived at the place of complete peace and confidence? Then there's my sweet little mustard-seed faith in the passenger seat whispering, *Be patient.* Somewhere in the distance my future is waiting while I muster enough strength to finally get my life moving. Meanwhile, my present is frozen behind the steering wheel, trying to determine if I can perform under these conditions.

No one ends up stagnant in life because they want to be. We end up stagnant in life because the unknown is scary. Subconsciously we believe that choosing to live in a perpetual state of indecision is better than making the wrong decision.

Indecision is defined as the inability to make a decision quickly. It's easy to move quickly when you aren't burdened down, but when you are heavy, you can't move as quickly. More than anything, what weighs us down internally are the thoughts that our fear, shame, past, and insecurities create. If we could peek inside the mind of a person experiencing indecision, we would see that, generally, they aren't suffering from a lack of vision but rather the cloudiness that comes with playing out too many potential outcomes of that vision. Eventually everything becomes cloudy, and they lose the passion, creativity, and precision necessary to activate their next step.

If you read those last sentences and said "Amen!" then you can relate completely to the mental exhaustion that comes with navigating the thoughts, emotions, and questions that come with being stuck.

Will it be worth it? Do I have what it takes? Can I get it done? Do I open up, or do I remain closed? Do I try again, or do I avoid the pain of disappointment? Do I stay or do I go? If you've ever found yourself weighing any of the aforementioned thoughts or questions regarding your life, it's not as simple as comparing two options. The endless potential consequences of those options play out in your mind until all you want to do is nothing at all.

The mind becomes the arena where thoughts duel to the finish. Each thought competes to take the lead and run our lives. We think one day the competition will reveal a winner, but in reality it's a never-ending battle until we actively intervene and make a decision.

The whirlwind of thoughts often blinds us from recognizing that they really have only two origins: they are birthed either from our faith or from our fear. Our fears pretend to keep us safe. Our faith demands we draw on courage we aren't sure we possess. If fear didn't feel so comfortable, and faith wasn't so expensive, indecision would vanish, and confidence would emerge.

What do you do when fear and faith speak to you at the same time? The answer to this question for many is simple: nothing. We often find a way to accept the duality of fear and faith as normal and, therefore, continue to live conflicted and stuck. Interestingly, from the outside looking in, you'd never be able to tell someone is stuck. Most of us can go about our daily routines: working, cooking, posting, loving, laughing, socializing, and producing as if nothing is wrong. We become envious of other people who seemingly do not struggle with being decisive. Of course, just because it seems like someone can make tough decisions doesn't mean their life is progressing. True progression can only be accurately gauged by how a person has expanded in wisdom, knowledge, and vulnerability on the inside, not what they have amassed externally.

I've always imagined that when people are taking a leap of faith, they're taking off from one cliff to another. Like watching a movie, I can imagine their legs spread wide, heart full of faith, and spirit full of determination as they pursue the destination ahead of them. While it's dramatic and scenic, I've been envisioning it all wrong.

A true leap of faith doesn't have a valley separating us from our next destination. But we do have to leap over a heap of fear and insecurity. As much as we want to possess the type of faith that allows us to take off with no problem, what if we land smack-dab in the middle of our worst fears? I can't tell you how many times I've had conversations with people who wanted to move, leave their jobs, start a business, go back to school, or take countless leaps of faith but were too afraid they wouldn't be successful. They looked at all the fear-based outcomes that could occur and chose to stay still instead of leap. Staying still would've been easy, but on the inside they couldn't quiet the voice of faith daring them to take a leap.

That's why we must pay close attention to what is taking place inside of our souls. If we've found ourselves unable to choose faith over fear, then we know about the hunger that accompanies those stagnant moments. On the inside, we are hungry for more and longing for a consistent state of fulfillment in every area of our lives. That hunger and longing is our spirit shaking up our complacency so we can become desperate for the more that has been assigned to our names.

KNOW YOUR ENVIRONMENT

I'm giving you permission to stop berating yourself for not being able to push forward. Instead, dissect your thoughts to help you discover the beauty in the unknown.

But before we get started, I need you to understand that trust in the unknown is not the result of having answers to every question that plagues your mind. Trust in the unknown is a belief that progress and unanswered questions *can* coexist. When you don't believe the two can coexist, you're not trapped because you don't want to grow—you're trapped because you think you need all the answers before you can move forward.

Instead of focusing on the what-ifs, my goal is to help you understand how your thoughts control your actions so you can determine which thoughts are worthy of taking up real estate in your mind.

To analyze our thoughts, we must consider the environment that produced them in the first place. Thoughts are seeds. When tended to properly, those thoughts begin to take root and ultimately produce fruit. The fruit is our actions—the essence of our existence and how we present ourselves to the world around us. Our character, confidence, integrity, loyalty, and work ethic (or lack thereof) all derive from thoughts that began as mere seeds.

The process from thought to seed to fruit is a cycle. That cycle is the same whether we're teenaged or middle-aged. The environment determines whether the cycle benefits or destroys us. Environment comes from the French word *environ*, which means "surrounding." Any botanist will tell you that certain plants cannot grow in certain environments. That's why it's important to recognize the environment, or the surroundings, that cultivated the thought.

You know your thoughts, and maybe you even know your actions, but have you considered your environment and how it's contributed to your thoughts and actions?

Humanity began as a thought in God's mind. But before He planted us, He formed the environment because He recognized that for us to thrive, we'd need to be in surroundings that would allow us to flourish.

When the serpent engaged Eve, it appears he simply tried to get her to eat fruit. But his ultimate goal was to overthrow the environment God created.

Genesis 3:1 tells us everything we need to know about how the serpent was able to derail the woman from staying planted in the purpose God gave her. The New King James Version reads: "Now the serpent was more cunning than any beast of the field which the LORD God had made. And he said to the woman, 'Has God indeed said, "You shall not eat of every tree of the garden"'?"

I don't know about you, but when I seek to define the word *cunning*, I envision villains from suspense/thriller movies I've seen. I'm talking Anthony Hopkins as in the movie-*Fracture*-type villains. With this definition in mind, I feel like the serpent should have disguised the fruit in another fruit, or maybe tricked the woman while she was sleeping. But he didn't use any of the tricks I expected. Instead, he used the woman's mind against her by injecting a question that destabilized her world.

Let's reread that sentence.

Instead, he used the woman's mind against her by injecting a question that destabilized her world.

The serpent used the woman's mind against her. He injected a question that changed everything she knew. That one question changed her environment.

We spend *a lot* of time talking about external forces working against us, but I want to challenge you to consider that perhaps your greatest enemy lies between your ears.

Have you ever considered that your mind could be working against you and not for you? If your thoughts aren't helping you become wiser, more compassionate, focused, and disciplined, then what is it making you become? The serpent doesn't need to use any of the fancy tricks depicted in the movies because the power of this one question is enough for Eve's mind to start inching further and further away from God's vision for her life.

We all know the story. Eve told the serpent that they were allowed to eat the fruit from any tree in the garden, except one: the tree in the middle. In fact, they were not even to touch it, or they would die. But, long story short, the serpent's line of questioning changed the environment of her mind, moving her from the certainty of what she believed God said to uncertainty. She took some fruit and ate it. Not only that, she gave some to her husband, and he ate it too.

When given the opportunity to explain to God what happened when she ate from the tree, Genesis 3:13 tells us that Eve said, "The serpent deceived me, and I ate." *Strong's Concordance* explains that the word *deceived* in the original Hebrew manuscript was actually *naw-shaw'*, a primitive root meaning "to lead astray, i.e., (mentally) to delude, or (morally) to seduce, beguile, deceive greatly, utterly." It's easy to think of Eve as foolish when we regard her decision as a split-second one, but Eve was telling us in her own words that the journey from disciplined, safe, and protected didn't just happen overnight—it was a process. She reveals to us the seduction of sabotage.

Sabotage is slow, stealthy, and patient. It doesn't need immediate results. It only needs a small corner of your heart, mind, or soul. Sabotage pokes a pin-sized hole in your faith, then waits patiently for it to completely deflate. Eve eating from the fruit was the final act, but the play began the moment the serpent poked a hole in what Eve held as truth. The more time she focused on what the serpent said, the less time she focused on God's truth.

The woman corrected the serpent with what she understood as the truth, but eventually she abandoned that truth to test the answer the enemy proposed. Eve wasn't even thinking about the fruit until the serpent asked that question.

I propose that the environment that produced the negative, distracting thoughts that exist in your mind originated from an unanswered question that invaded your soul.

IS GOD GOOD?

Before Eve had the encounter with the serpent, all she knew was the environment God created for her. Genesis tells us over and over again in chapter 1 that the environment was good. All Eve knew was goodness. She didn't have to question whether or not God was good because everything in her world spoke to His goodness, until it didn't. That moment in Genesis 3 is so monumental because it's the first time Eve must consider whether or not God is actually good. The serpent would have her believe that she and Adam are forbidden from eating the fruit because God is withholding greater knowledge from them.

What do you do when experiences make you question whether God is good? Some of us are far too religious to ever truly admit it, but there are moments when we aren't so sure anymore. Of course, we don't want to appear ungrateful, but when we're burying a loved one, facing abuse, fighting a disease, or scraping resources together just to keep a roof over our head, a small corner of our soul wonders, "Is God good?" If Jesus, hanging on the cross, asked God, "How could you forsake me?" then there are moments when our human experiences and divine pursuits clash with such violence that we have no choice but to wonder where our good God is.

The cunning serpent didn't have to force Eve to eat the fruit any more than he had to force you or me to make the choices we've made. All he had to do to change Eve's diet was change her environment by making her question the goodness of God. Eve went from a woman surrounded by the knowledge of who God created her to be in a world He created her to dominate, to a woman whose thoughts about God, her world, and her identity were changed, all because of a question. That one question didn't just change her thoughts and then ultimately her actions; that one question changed the thoughts and actions of every generation that would come through her.

There will never be a generation afforded the safe haven of exclusive goodness that Eve experienced in the garden. Instead, we're born into a world where questioning the goodness of God is natural, and establishing and maintaining faith requires a fight.

Working It Out

If you're ready to dig in to this with me, and I hope that you are, you'll need to access the parts of you that you don't often take the time to explore. In this case, that place in your heart that still feels unsure and heavy no matter how much you've grown in your faith. We need to explore the thoughts that environment produced, as well as the place where you began questioning God's goodness, your goodness, and the goodness of this world. The easiest, and scariest, place we will venture to is the place in our history where we first experienced unsettling disappointment.

If I asked you to tell me your thoughts connected to feeling afraid, devalued, and ashamed, you could likely list those with awkward ease. After all, a version of those thoughts runs fiercely and quietly in your mind throughout the day.

This moment isn't about attacking those thoughts. Remember? I want us to examine the environment that nurtured and nourished those thoughts. Go deep enough to discover the question that de-stabilized you in the first place. What question has your soul been trying to answer? When did you get stuck on a merry-go-round? Let's attack that environment together.

If you're not in a quiet space right now, it may be more benefi-cial to do this exercise when you have time to truly take a minute to yourself. Charlotte Stallings, a woman I deeply admire, taught me a breathing technique I'd like you to use for this moment.

1. Inhale like you're smelling roses and exhale like you're blow-ing out a candle.
2. Do that three times.
3. Become one with your thoughts, emotions, and spirit, bring-ing them together and into focus.
4. As you hop into your internal time machine, drive down memory lane.
5. Keep breathing.
6. Go back to a moment that stands out in your mind as when you felt the most stuck. It could be ten years ago or an hour ago. Found it?
7. Paint a picture in your head of your life in that moment. Who were your friends? Where were you living? How were you wear-ing your hair? (We always remember our hair phases.) Embody that version of yourself. Feel those fears and hopes again. Allow those bright, scary, beautiful emotions to come back to you.
8. Breathe in and breathe out as who you were then comes into focus. Now, ask yourself one simple question: What did I need to know? If you've been using a journal to accompany

your thoughts, write down those things you needed to know. Personally, I needed to know I was safe. I needed to know I wasn't alone. I needed to know I was loved. I needed to know that it was okay to still have hope.

9. Next question: When was the first time you needed to know those things?

I'll go first. When I began telling my story, I usually started with my teen pregnancy. That was the moment I deemed as my greatest shift. I was wrong. When I was seven years old, my father, a pastor, felt led to move our church from West Virginia to Texas. There were many striking differences between Dallas, Texas, and Charleston, West Virginia, but the one that stands out most in my mind twenty-five-plus years later occurred on our first Sunday in Dallas. Every Sunday in West Virginia, we sat with my mom. When we moved to Dallas, our seating arrangement changed. My parents sat on the platform behind the pulpit with the other pastors while my siblings and I sat with the congregation. Our church in West Virginia was a family church where everyone knew one another. Our first Sunday in Dallas we had 1,500 visitors!

I can still remember the sense of rejection, loneliness, and isolation I felt without my mom in that room full of people. When I look back at that moment as an adult, I don't see it as a big deal, but the mere fact that I remember it vividly is a sign that it affected me in a deep way.

Sometimes we look at moments in our history as small or inconsequential compared to the things other people face, but when something wounds you, it doesn't matter whether it would've wounded someone else. It's not wise to compare or minimize our pain because it doesn't feel significant compared to that of others. When we do this, we run the risk of not recognizing the moment that destabilized our confidence and identity.

For me, this small, seemingly insignificant moment in church was when I first began to question my worth and value in my world. "Do I belong here?" That question became the environment where my thoughts lived. Confidence couldn't survive in that environment of uncertainty. Faith couldn't establish roots with so much doubt beaming down. The only things that could thrive in that environment were insecurity, rejection, pain, and fear. I lived in that environment for so long that it became my mind's norm. I didn't realize my soul was still desperately trying to answer that question. I believed my actions were my own, but they were being fueled by the ache of questioning whether I belonged.

I clung to any friendship, relationship, or opportunity that appeared to have the answer to that question. If I didn't fit into those friendships, relationships, or opportunities by being myself, I invented a version of me who could fit. There was no limit to how far I was willing to go to finally put that question to rest. See how that one question altered my thoughts and then those thoughts affected my actions? Subsequently, those actions painted a reality—one that left me feeling fearful, ashamed, and weak. That cycle continued until one day when I stopped taking actions based on what I thought and instead began to activate the knowledge I possessed.

GAINING CONFIDENCE

I want you to be confident, but not with a superficial confidence based on repeating a phrase over and over again in your mind.

I want you to be confident because there are some things on the inside of your spirit that you know that you know.

Don't accept complacency with the unsure and insecure areas of your life. Attack that insecurity head-on because you recognize it's keeping you from the security you need to gain authentic confidence.

Confidence is the result of not only thinking good thoughts but also of knowing truth and allowing that truth to change the way you show up in the world and improve your interaction with others.

My goal is to help you realize not only who you are but who you are in God. If I left you at discovering who you are, you may have moments when another question could invade your mind and derail your progress; however, if I can help you realize who you are in God, the questions will come, but you will finally have an answer.

If you're a fan of Oprah, or just an avid member of any social media platform, you've likely seen a quote from civil rights activist, poet, and author Maya Angelou: "Do the best you can until you know better. Then when you know better, do better." For some time I struggled with this quote because I recognized how often my inner Eve knew better but I didn't do better. I underestimated the power of truly knowing something versus thinking something.

My inner Eve struggled because she thought better but never turned what she thought into what she knew. It's one thing to *think* you deserve better, and another to *know* you deserve better.

When you begin to transform what you think into what you know, your actions will have no choice but to fall in line. Your actions are a direct reflection of what's taking place in your mind.

For instance, when I begin *thinking* I should lose weight, I work out in the morning and eat cake at night. When I start *knowing* I should lose weight, I work out, and I cut out sugar, carbs, and fried foods from my diet. Knowing flips a switch that allows me to resist the temptation of living as if I don't know better.

Knowing produces doing. If you're not doing, then conflicting thoughts in your mind are keeping you from activating what you know.

When I mentor women, I've noticed how they often explain how they feel or what they believe and then conclude by saying, "I don't know." Essentially, they know, because they've just told me, but with that one statement they rob themselves of the ability to *know* what they actually know. Whether it's due to a toxic relationship, an issue at work, or uncertainty about tomorrow, if you're one of those "I don't know"-ers, consider this a personal challenge. Stop presenting your truth, feelings, and emotions and then dismissing them with "I don't know." Stop introducing a phrase that leaves room for uncertainty within your soul. There are going to be plenty of things that you truly don't know; don't add what you *do* know to that list.

By the way, expressing what you know doesn't confine you to living in that space for the rest of your life. Sometimes we're afraid to say what we know because we don't believe that we will still have room to grow, change, and evolve. Transformation needs a starting point. We need to understand and be confident with what we know so we can begin the journey of discovering what we don't know.

This book is about becoming more effective in discovering the version of you that God created to revolutionize the world. The serpent robbed Eve of her knowledge, but the serpent could not keep her from acquiring knowledge. Eve could have stayed planted in the field of her disappointment and shame. The serpent probably hoped that Eve would stay stuck there. We know that he desired for that one moment in the garden to disconnect her from God forever.

Little did he know that God would not leave His creation without an opportunity to transform their knowledge. Eve knew what she did, but she also knew what God said. Eve held on to what God said when she was cast out of the garden. She hung on to what God said even when she had to live with the consequences of her actions. Eve didn't simply allow what God said to become the compass from which she lived her life; she regained control of her mind.

Eve is my homegirl because she found a way to move beyond what happened to her to again become a good partner with God on the earth.

YOU ARE KNOWN

I don't know what forbidden fruit or disastrous question has entered your mind. I don't know what made you feel fragile on the inside, but I do know that before any of those things happened, God desired to partner with you on the earth. He still knows you are worthy even if you don't see it. He still knows you can break generational curses and change the paradigms of your family or community culture. He still knows that you can subdue and have dominion.

In Jeremiah 29:11, God gives us insight into how much He knows about His creation: "'For I know the plans I have for you,' declares the LORD, 'plans to prosper you and not to harm you, plans to give you hope and a future'" (NIV).

Did you notice the word *know*? God is telling His prophet in this text that He doesn't just wonder about His plans for us, He *knows* them. The question is, do you want to discover what God knows more than you want to be stuck in what you think? Are you willing to bench your thoughts and begin pursuing what God knows? If you can commit to pursuing God, your life will have no choice but to be revolutionized.

If you're reading this, then there are some things you've known for a while. You've known that you need to get therapy. Or you've known that you need to leave that relationship. You've known that you need to take better care of your health. You've known that you need to be more disciplined with your time. You've known these things for so long that it's easier to ignore them than it is to activate and do something about them.

I am praying right now that as you read and process your thoughts, God would begin to highlight the area of your life where you have been so distracted by the thoughts themselves that you can't activate what you know. My experience with God has taught me that the more I activate what I know, the more He gives me vision and clarity for the unknown.

THREE

EYES WIDE OPEN

Then the eyes of both of them were opened, and they knew that they were naked; and they sewed fig leaves together and made themselves coverings.

—GENESIS 3:7

Have you ever been watching a scary movie and instinctively closed your eyes when the frightening part was coming because you just didn't want to see it? If so, in that moment, were you afraid that you would miss out on something and the plot would no longer make sense? I doubt it. Usually the only important thing in that moment is that you protect yourself from having terrifying images etched in your mind. Closing our eyes often seems like the only way we can possibly survive the big and scary.

We aren't born with the innate ability to predict when a movie is going to display a scene that we'd rather not see. Our experience with films, and the way they generally progress, helps us use our instincts to avoid seeing something we'd rather not see. Once you've become accustomed to not giving yourself permission to look at what scares you, it's hard to break the rhythm of closing your eyes when it comes on. If your life were a movie, this pattern would be fine, but when we close our eyes to what scares us in real life, we miss the opportunity to live fearlessly.

Avoiding what scares you means that what scares you is in control of you.

Not long ago my husband got a motorcycle. He watched every YouTube video he could find about operating the bike. He read the owner's manual, took the courses, and practiced riding back and forth in our driveway. Eventually, he ventured outside of the driveway. Little by little he extended his distance, but he was intentional about not getting on the highway. He mapped out his routes before leaving the house to make sure that he could avoid the highway and still reach his destination. I know eventually he will get on the highway, but for now, because his knowledge of the bike is so limited, he's not ready to be that vulnerable. That caution now controls how he functions and navigates when riding his bike.

This is what happens to us when we're controlled by what we don't want to see again. It's why I couldn't recognize that moment when I was seven years old and missing the comfort of sitting next to my mother in church as a trauma. There was a part of me that closed my eyes to that moment because I didn't want to remember it. Yet my desire not to feel that way again controlled how I would change my personality depending on the room I entered.

In chapter 2, I hope you could identify the event when your environment shifted, which changed your thoughts and then your actions. In preparing to lay the framework for moving forward, consider how what you've experienced has affected what you believe. Additionally, I will discuss how you can create a plan to tackle the things you have yet to experience.

GOOD AND EVIL

Some things are undeniably evil. If you need an example, just turn on the news and check out any of the top stories. Murder, rape, abuse, terrorism, racism, and so many other forms of darkness are constantly being shown. Without fail, somewhere in the discussion someone asks a question attempting to make peace with how God could allow certain things to happen.

I found the answer in the garden.

When Adam and Eve ate from the forbidden fruit, Genesis tells us that their eyes were opened. Nothing in the text suggests that Adam or Eve were created physically blind; however, the moment they ate from the fruit is clearly defined as a moment when something in them went from being blind to being aware.

We generally attribute the fall of humanity to Eve eating fruit from a forbidden tree. The tree, however, had a name: the Tree of the Knowledge of Good and Evil. "But of the tree of the knowledge of good and evil you shall not eat, for in the day that you eat of it you shall surely die" (Genesis 2:17).

Before they ate from this tree, they had no knowledge of good and evil. All they had was their reality. They saw their reality as neither good nor evil—it was just theirs.

For some reason, God did not want humanity to have the knowledge of good and evil. God didn't want you to be able to look at your body as good or look at your failures as evil. He didn't want you to be able to look at those who hurt you, or whom you hurt, as evil. He didn't even want you to see those who helped you as good. He desired for us to have an existence that wasn't restricted to categories.

Unfortunately that ship has sailed, and now we're living in a world where we see too much of almost everything.

In 2020, a black man by the name of George Floyd was killed by a Minneapolis police officer. The officer, Derek Chauvin, claimed that Floyd was resisting arrest. In an effort to restrain him, he laid Floyd on his stomach, on the ground, and pinned his knee to the back of his neck. For eight minutes and forty-six seconds, Floyd pleaded with the officer to release him. He cried out for his dead mother. He repeated the words *I can't breathe!* until he took his very last breath. The video showing his death went viral.

Social media was ablaze with righteous indignation about Floyd's death and the systemic racism and dehumanization that has plagued the black community for centuries. The beauty and frustration of social media is that you're not engaging exclusively with people who look like you. Instead, just a click away is a barrage of personalities with viewpoints that can create internal conflict and dialogue that affect your mental and emotional well-being.

That's exactly what happened as I went down that rabbit hole of people sharing their thoughts about the death of George Floyd. I was exposed to so many articles that discouraged, enraged, or disappointed me that eventually I had to make a decision to stop seeking opinions and viewpoints that upset me. I came to a point when I realized I wasn't following those people for a reason and I didn't want to continue exposing myself to that level of rhetoric.

I had an epiphany in the middle of a mental argument with myself about the latest content I'd just read. As I was thinking, *How could someone even say something like that?* it suddenly occurred to me that I was never supposed to see it in the first place. I had been searching out conversations that I knew would upset me when I could have just been a faithful member of "Mind Your Business Ministries." I started judging "those" people because I didn't agree with them. In my mind, I thought of them as evil and myself as good. That realization changed the way I consumed social media.

The beauty and the complexity of social media is that there is a diversity of thought. I've learned to limit my exposure to social media so I have space to intentionally dissect my own thoughts before being swarmed by so many different opinions. I now realize there are some pockets of the internet I must avoid at all costs for the sake of my mental, emotional, and spiritual state.

The other thing that happened to Adam and Eve when their eyes were opened was that they saw they were naked. This gives us insight into how the knowledge of good and evil affected how they saw themselves. Before eating from the tree, they were naked, but they didn't see that as problematic. After they ate from the tree, they saw their nakedness and judged it as wrong.

They were never supposed to see their vulnerability as something to be ashamed of.

I wonder what else we were never meant to see. That's now how I view the atrocities that have taken place in the world. I don't see them as things God allowed. I see them as things God never wanted us to see.

God did not intend for there to be slavery, racism, murder, hate, cancer, or death. Evil existed, as evidenced by the serpent in the garden, but evil didn't have anything in its environment until Eve subjected herself to it by eating the fruit. What was done cannot be undone, but Romans 8:28 details how God can use all things to get them back to good: "And we know that all things work together for good to those who love God, to those who are the called according to His purpose." It doesn't mean that all things start as good, but that all things can get back to good with work. That's what you're doing right now. You're learning how to allow God to work in your life until He's able to look at it and be reminded of the most repeated phrase in Genesis 1: "God saw that it was good."

How, then, do we prepare ourselves for the next batch of things that are bound to come our way that we were never meant to see? You come to a place where you can control, contain, and compare what you see.

Perhaps when you saw that word *compare* you were like, "But, sis, you just told us to not compare ourselves." I know. I know. Just keep an open mind, and I'll explain it in more detail.

Let's begin with control.

CONTROL (AND REPLACE)

Our eyes are opened to everything good and bad. There's nothing we can do to change it now, so we must learn to navigate the world we're in. Fitness enthusiasts who train people to no longer have muffin tops, make healthy lifestyle changes, and avoid thigh chafing say the first step in changing your diet is to throw out all the bad stuff. Allegedly the more work it takes to eat badly, the more it deters you from eating badly. I tried this once, and it's true. I definitely didn't go out of my way to eat bad things when they weren't within reach. (Just as a sidebar, if you're considering doing this, I did have a major attitude when I had only salad in my fridge. That's not the point though.) The point is discipline doesn't always come, if when faced with two options, we're able to choose the better option. Sometimes discipline comes when we're not given any options to begin with.

That makes sense with a diet, but let's talk about how that plays out in other areas of our life. My decision to no longer seek out the commentary and agendas that upset me regarding the George

Floyd case was an intentional decision to maintain my focus on equality and justice. When I focused my attention and time on the people who typically don't express concern for the racial inequities of America, yet were speaking out for the first time, I felt hopeful and optimistic that change can occur. That was opposed to the comments I was reading in social media that made me feel like no matter how much progress we make, we'll always be behind.

Like a premature baby in need of special attention to survive, I needed to incubate my hope. I could not allow it to be exposed to commentary that would knock me off-center. As you begin to incubate yourself for this transformation, it's important that you be disciplined about more than just what you think. You need to incubate what you allow yourself to see too.

Emphasis on the phrase *what you allow.*

Some things are going to happen that are ultimately out of your control. I'm not referring to those things. Focus on the willful moments when we open ourselves to take in content that weakens our will to become whole. If you're trying to discover who you are after a breakup, then stalking the ex is only going to cause you more trauma. You don't need to know who he's talking to now or how his life has progressed at the expense of you stagnating.

The same is true if you're trying to save money. You may have to unsubscribe from marketing emails targeting your bank account. If we aren't careful, we will subject ourselves to a narrative that suggests our maturity is contingent on the ability to say no to meals when we're trying to lose weight, to remain friends after a breakup, or to go shopping without dipping into our savings. Maturity is not just being able to say no; it's also about making sure that you're not in a position that makes you waver in the first place. When you recognize that what you subject yourself to truly plays a role in who you can become, you become more diligent about protecting yourself from what you see, read, and listen to.

When you've subscribed to a negative narrative for a long time, changing can be hard, but it's worth it. One of the most powerful scriptures I've read about God details how He sees the transgressions of His creation: "I, even I, am He who blots out your transgressions for My own sake; / And I will not remember your sins." Isaiah 43:25 confirms that for Him to maintain His identity as the holy God, He doesn't allow himself to see where we've missed the mark.

God is talking about controlling His sight to maintain His identity. The scripture is clear that He doesn't blot out our transgressions for our benefit, but He does it "for My own sake." We're created in God's image, and if we want to truly strive to be like Him, then we must come to a place where we commit to controlling our sight to protect our identity. What are you consuming with your eyes that deflates your momentum? Whatever it is, I challenge you to become an active participant in your growth by no longer waiting until you have the strength to take it all in but, instead, giving yourself only one direction to look.

This doesn't just apply to how you see the world around you, but also how you see your journey. You have to be willing to see yourself as more than your past. Every attempt I made at moving forward in life was thwarted because I couldn't see beyond my shame. I didn't think it was possible for me to have made a mistake and still be a "good girl." I only saw myself as a broken person, and so that's all I became. My ability to identify and celebrate my goodness allowed me to look beyond the moments when I knew better but didn't do better. I guess you can say I started listening to that voice inside me.

If we're going to keep things completely transparent in this book, we should admit that there's usually a voice inside us that tries to nudge us when we know we're looking at something that we shouldn't. Listen to that voice. That voice is trying to help you. Fortunately for you, I'm not just asking you to control what you see by listing the ways that you must become blind. Instead, I want to challenge you to take it one step further and replace what you *were* seeing with images that motivate you to become.

Oh em gee—this is getting good!

It's one thing to control what you see, but there's another level of growth that comes when you replace it. Sure, we can throw all the garbage out of the pantry, but if we don't replace it with something that is actually beneficial at keeping us on track, we'll return to our old habits. When I threw away that junk food and was stuck with salad, your girl was struggling. When I threw away that junk and replaced it with delicious and healthy recipes, your girl was thriving. When what is ahead of you is greater than what is behind you, you can walk away from that which no longer serves.

Working It Out

Grab that journal you've been using and let's reverse engineer this thing.

1. What do you want to see in your life that you currently don't see?

   Before you get started about the cars, houses, or relationships, let's begin with you as a person. There's a difference between saying "I want to lose twenty pounds" and saying "I want to become more disciplined." It's easier to maintain a conviction to change when we have a goal rooted in who we want to become versus what we want to have.

2. How will you feel when you achieve that goal?

Identifying what success feels like is important. If we focus exclusively on what success looks like, we can be deterred, especially if we feel we have a long way to go before realizing that vision. If feeling successful at becoming more disciplined makes you feel confident, then the moment you make one disciplined decision, that seed of confidence is one step closer to producing tangible fruit.

3. Now for the hard question: What's keeping you from achieving that goal?

Sometimes we aren't motivated to do the work to achieve our goal because the full realization of it requires more discipline or work than we have to give. You don't have to pay in full to start working toward your goal today. It's very rare that someone purchases a car or home and has all the money up front. More times than not, a person makes a down payment and then begins to make regular payments until they own what they were pursuing in the first place. You don't have the motivation, energy, faith, or discipline to radically transform your life all at once—no one does. All you need is enough for a down payment. The more we see our culture decrease the turnaround for gratification, the more impatient we become when we don't see our lives begin to move as quickly as we'd like. Your goal isn't as far off as you think it is, but it will only continue to be pushed further and further away if you aren't able to muster the courage you need to start today.

A Special Note

Before I close out this subject of controlling and replacing what we see, let's fess up to something we all struggle with: how we view our bodies. This begins with the understanding that every part of us, from the inside out, has been awakened to the knowledge of good and evil. We see certain parts of our bodies, and we think to ourselves, *Good!* Then we see another part of our bodies and say, "Evil!" We cannot compartmentalize ourselves like that. God created us as a beautiful mosaic of peaks and valleys, highs and lows.

There have been moments when I've caught a glimpse of my body in the mirror and a part of me grieved that the area wasn't tauter and more defined. I know I'm not the only one who has been there. The grief in that moment is how our confidence shrivels and dies. The good news is that our confidence can come back to life. The next time you look in the mirror and your old way of looking at your body begins to cue the music for the funeral procession for your confidence, pull the cord and survey every inch of your body until you find something to love. Girl, if you can't start with nothing but a small mole, you better work that mole! Name that mole. Tell that mole she's beautiful. Lotion that mole up and let her shine. I don't care how long your confidence has been dead, it can always be resurrected. You can even start researching body-positivity blogs and influencers who can help you jump-start your journey. There's an influencer for every shape and size.

I've been practicing this in my own life. When my skin goes on its monthly time travel back to adolescent puberty, I look in the mirror, and my initial thoughts are about how ugly, bad, or just downright evil my pimples are. Immediately I force myself to stop thinking negatively about myself and replace that thought with something that makes me feel good.

Activate this rhythm in your life. Control the negative narrative by stopping it in its tracks. Replace the negative narrative with a higher thought of the beauty God created when He made you.

CONTAIN (AND EMBRACE)

Controlling what we allow to take up space in our vision limits unnecessary exposure to things that weaken our progress. What do we do with the moments that invade the bubble we're creating? This is where containment comes in.

In March 2020, the same year George Floyd was murdered, the world also experienced the COVID-19 pandemic. The spread of the novel coronavirus was far and wide. Immediately, governments around the world began placing restrictions on how citizens could engage and gather. Seemingly overnight the world began resembling a science-fiction film. People began wearing masks. Everyone was expected to maintain a six-foot distance at all times. Only businesses deemed essential were able to remain open, and public gatherings were prohibited.

I thought that it would go away as quickly as it came, that the spread of the virus would be contained, and that life would return to normal by July, when I was planning to host a conference. As the weeks passed, I witnessed events of all types transition from in-person to virtual. The more it became clear that I wouldn't be able to host the conference, the more upset I became. It didn't matter that my husband had been leading our church through online-only services for months. Selfishly, I felt entitled for my plans to be unscathed by the consequences of the shutdown.

As I was sorting through my emotions, I started thinking about the many people who have become my mentors and heroes. They had incredible survival stories about facing cancer, bankruptcy, disloyalty, and so much more. All were forced to see things they didn't want to see. I realized that I was praying for the same testimony of strength and survival to be on my life as I'd witnessed on theirs, but I didn't want the struggle that produces the strength.

Sis, your girl just preached!

When people commend others on their strength, it's because they made it look easy—but when you're the one earning the strength, you become intimately acquainted with the struggle.

I knew I was going to have to face all the emotional and practical implications of postponing the conference. As I was faced with releasing volunteers, refunding customers, and warring with vendors, I couldn't help but begin to feel like I'd failed in some way. I was beating myself up for not being prepared for the unknown.

I started thinking about all the things I should have done differently, but then I remembered a very deep and powerful mantra my father shares with us often: "You don't know until you know." It doesn't seem that deep when I type it out, but I promise you this saying has rung so true in my life. When we are confronted with things we don't see (or we'd rather not see), we're strengthened and prepared to know better the next time around.

Have you ever had one of those random urges to declutter your kitchen? You find yourself at the local dollar store or Container Store so you can purchase containers to make your shelves look more uniform. The flour, sugar, oatmeal, and pasta all come in their own packaging. It looks great in the store but cluttered in our pantries. So we take the items out of their original packaging and place them in matching containers with labels. We repeat this process until our shelves have gone from chaos to order.

That's essentially what I want you to do with your life.

As you take in and process what's happening around you, organize and place your thoughts and emotions in appropriately sized containers with accurate labels so that they are not scattered about. Pay special attention to those boxes that already have a label, as many of them may need to be repackaged.

For instance, my experience with postponing the conference came in a package that initially felt like anxiety and failure. I could have left that in its original package and decided to not categorize it properly, but I knew that would eat away at me on the inside. I married my admiration for my mentors with the experience and placed it in a new container labeled "Necessary for growth." By seeing it properly, I was able to embrace it even though it was a struggle.

Containing our thoughts and emotions is not the same as repressing them. Containing our emotions is an opportunity to have self-intimacy. Self-intimacy allows us to give God access to the most tender, frustrated, broken parts of ourselves. If we don't acknowledge how what we see wounds us, then we can go to church every week but never truly encounter God. Conversely, when we make a practice of breaking our hearts open, we could never step foot in a church and not encounter God in a deep way.

That's when we move from just containing to embracing. It's not unusual for us to exclusively want to embrace that which makes us feel nice, warm, and fuzzy. What's more challenging is embracing the twists and turns of life. Who could blame us for that? In an effort to protect us, our brains communicate that embracing the twists and turns could result in us becoming disoriented. One thing I learned quickly when navigating Los Angeles is that sometimes the only way to avoid being stuck in LA traffic is to learn how to maneuver through the canyons.

For a girl from Texas who is used to only flat roads, navigating the canyons seemed daunting. The lanes are generally narrow, the turns are sudden, and there are very few road signs. You know what else I learned? You can't discover the best views of the city unless you're willing to brave the mountains.

The same is true for your life, my friend. When you begin this journey of embracing what you didn't want to see, it won't always feel good. Sometimes it will be downright scary and uncomfortable. That's okay. You can keep moving even in the scary and uncomfortable. You will come to a place where you look back over your life and you recognize that your development didn't take place because everything went the right way. No, when you take inventory of your life, you will see that you were developed because you went through the fire and came out more refined.

Working It Out

I have an exercise for the next time you're staring down a circumstance that you'd rather not see. I won't lie, this is going to sound kind of bold and crazy, but it's going to help you stretch your mind. Start asking yourself, *I wonder what good could come of this?* This isn't a question you ask yourself when first confronted with your trauma. This is a question that should be reserved for when you dare to peek beyond where you are and begin to question where you could be headed. If you can begin to ascertain even the smallest particle of goodness in a dark season, imagine what God can do.

When recovering from the loss of a loved one, it may mean extracting the virtues of the life you're mourning and allowing them to live on in you. When grappling with a business that has gone under, it may mean assessing how you could build your teams or leadership style differently. You may have to stretch yourself into the land of impossible to try to imagine what could come of your trauma, but stretching your mind makes room for the impossible.

I'm reminded of Ephesians 3:20.

Paul wrote a letter to the church of Ephesus to help them establish themselves as a church, but in this verse he gives us insight into God's character. He closed this portion of his letter by writing, "Now to Him who is able to do exceedingly abundantly above all that we ask or think, according to the power that works in us." When we go beyond containing and into embracing, by playing out how what hurt us could potentially work to make us better, we exercise the divine power in us. From there, God breathes on it and takes it to the realm of exceedingly and abundantly. Then one day you'll look up and be able to embrace what you didn't want to see because you're now able to contain it properly.

A Special Note

As you've been reading this book, there may have been so many things that you did not want to see. Perhaps this book feels like the last lifeline you have left. I want to celebrate you for hanging on this long. So many other people would have given up by now, but you're still here even though it hasn't been easy. I guarantee you that the mountains you've climbed have undiscovered treasure. Your tenacity and perseverance are gifts this world so desperately needs. I pray one day you retrace your steps and share your tips on how to stay alive even after you've been wrecked.

COMPARE (AND RELEASE)

Comparing what you see has nothing to do with looking at the life of the people around you and everything to do with daring to see your life the way God does. It's probably the part of this process that is the easiest to explain yet the most difficult to implement. Comparing what you see comes down to stretching your faith to look beyond your perspective on your situation and circumstance and daring to ask God to show you what He sees. We're not really in any healthy relationship until we're willing to lay down our perspective and take on the perspective of the other person. To be honest, it's one of the most rewarding parts of marriage but also the most annoying. Yes, I said *annoying*. You see, the thing is, from my perspective, I'm totally right, and my husband is wrong.

When I begin to look from his perspective, while taking into account his personality, character, and life experiences, then my narrative changes a bit. That's when things get annoying. I can no longer hang on to my right when I see his right too.

One of the scriptures I see people quote quite often is 1 Samuel 16:7: "But the LORD said to Samuel, 'Do not look at his appearance or at his physical stature, because I have refused him. For the LORD does not see as man sees; for man looks at the outward appearance, but the LORD looks at the heart.'" We love to espouse that God looks at the heart, but we hardly ever go the extra mile to be like God in this way.

I can't think of a better scripture to unpack the beauty of comparison than 1 Samuel 16:7. This scripture is why we must be willing to step out of our feelings and emotions so that we can dare to ask God to soften our hearts. The ultimate goal is for us to come to a place where we can see people, circumstances, and opportunities the way that He sees them. This only works when we're willing to surrender our vision fully. You can't do this type of work if your agenda is to ultimately be right. This kind of work is only fruitful when you're willing to completely abandon your position to see from every angle; and to be successful in this, you need God.

When it comes to dealing with people, I ask God to show me the person's heart. The struggle with tense moments in relationships is that it often sweeps all the other moments under the rug. When my husband and I are having one of those moments in our marriage, I begin inwardly discussing his lack of appreciation or acknowledgment for who I am in his life. I have to force myself to stop fanning the flames of my anger and then ask God to remind me of my husband's heart. Suddenly an extinguisher is blown over my flame, and I'm left to deal with the true core of what has hurt me and the best way to communicate that from a place of love.

Comparing what I see to what God sees shows up differently when I'm looking at an opportunity versus a person. When a person is involved, it's easier to get a gauge on their heart, but when it's an opportunity, it's not always so straightforward. I make it a habit to ask myself, *Who will I have to become in order to pursue this opportunity, and is that person closer to or further away from who I'm supposed to be in God?* A deal may be lucrative, but if it requires me to sacrifice my relationships, morals, and character, it is the devil in disguise.

I learned to play dominoes with my uncles. You can imagine me being a young girl surrounded by older black men who trash-talked at the dominoes table as if they scored extra points for quips. Over and over again throughout the years I'd hear one saying in particular, "All money ain't good money." This saying always let me know that a play had been made that set up an opponent for defeat.

When we're comparing opportunities from our perspective versus God's, we must be willing to recognize that not every opportunity, no matter how good it looks on paper, is an opportunity that will produce the best version of ourselves. The right opportunity will not destroy the life God has given you, but it may change your life. Change and destruction are not the same thing, but change can become destruction if we don't navigate it with wisdom. The right opportunity may mean you have to strategize with the village around you to facilitate an environment for the opportunity to prosper, but if God is in the opportunity, then He's already buried provision to bring it to pass in your present.

I can't think of any better example for compare and release than when we see Jesus in the garden preparing for the cross. Matthew 26 gives us insight into Jesus' mindset beforehand. You can read the whole chapter to get the full context, but in layman's terms, I'm just going to tell you straight up: Jesus wondered if there was anyone else qualified who could be crucified instead of Him.

The chapter reveals to us that He didn't just leave it at that though. He took it a step further and released what He saw for what God the Father saw. Sometimes our pain, bitterness, and frustration sit with us so long that they become the only things we know. Believing that there is life beyond the pain requires so much faith that we'd rather stay tucked away in the darkness than risk having hope. As much as Jesus wanted to pass the cup, He also knew something else—there will be glory after this! Isn't it crazy how even with the promise of glory Jesus wanted to pass the cup?

Sometimes we think if we're promised an outcome that will ultimately allow us to marvel at the plans of God, we will endure anything that stands in our way with gladness. Yet we see Jesus struggling with the cup that was coming His way. If Jesus had to pray to get ready for the road ahead of Him, then we have to know there will be moments when we must do the same. You can know that you have glory on the way and still feel reluctant to face what's ahead of you, and that's okay. Every day is not meant to be easy, but every day can be a classroom, a learning experience that makes you better and wiser.

Working It Out

I must admit that I have always held my prayer life close to me. My sister is what one would call a prayer warrior. She has no problem opening her mouth and praying with power no matter where she is. I'm naturally a bit soft-spoken, and I haven't always felt confident in my faith, so prayer was something I reserved for my own quiet time or as meditation in my mind.

Prayer is an opportunity to be reminded of who God is and to bring our hearts into alignment with His purpose and will. It's not just the moment when we ask for what we need, but rather an opportunity to present ourselves fully. While some people are anointed to pray effortlessly, others need some guidance on the best way to open their hearts and invite God's presence within them.

There are four steps to open your heart in prayer. Let's look at them one step at a time.

1. **ADORATION.** We don't always live in the consciousness of our adoration for God, but bringing your mind into a space of acknowledging the fullness of who God is expands your mind. If you take a moment and really look at how incredible the earth is, you will have no choice but to honor God. The ocean didn't just come from nowhere. It was set in motion by a divine mind. When God set the ocean in motion, it never stopped moving. The brilliance of the stars, the heat the sun provides, the way all the earth works together to paint the most beautiful picture—it all began with God. I can then honor my life—that I began as a seed and became a being. How magnificent it is that God created a system for my heart to pump, my body to move, and my brain to be the command center of it all. No differently than when we meet someone and are inspired because of what they've done, adoration is an opportunity for us to recognize God's résumé. With His fullness in mind, words start coming to my mouth: "You are wonderful. You are majestic. You are a healer. You are a provider. You are perfect in all your ways. You are all-knowing."

2. **CONFESSION.** Prayer is the one place I can admit that I've fallen short, especially in comparison to who God is. I begin seeking forgiveness for complaining, doubting, bitterness, and frustration. In my humanity, I may be justified for those feelings, but in the presence of God I must consider what my actions communicate to Him. This is the space in which we bring all of ourselves to God.

3. **GRATITUDE.** Despite all the things I've done that have

missed the mark in some way, God still granted me relationships, opportunities, and revelations that could have been given to another person. This is thanksgiving. It's intentional moments of reflection that allow us to acknowledge God.

4. **INTERCESSION.** Intercession is when my will and God's will begin to wrestle. I make known the area of need that I have in my life. In that wrestling I don't just ask God to give me what I'd like, but I ask for God to qualify my desire in the first place. This is when we start saying things like, "God, if this isn't Your will for me, then take the desire away from me." When you go into prayer, you're armed with the promises and character of God. You can trust that God doesn't want to hurt you. He does not take joy in His creation suffering, and when God's creation suffers, it's because there is a greater glory that awaits them. The goal of prayer is to come out trusting there is glory that awaits you.

Prayer. It's the one sure way to find the release available in every situation—whether with people or circumstances. Use it to help open your eyes to God's truth.

A Special Note

Sometimes there are moments when I ask God to show me someone's heart, and He reveals to me that the person's heart needs God more than they need me.

Ummmm, bloop! That just gave somebody the freedom they needed.

The worst thing we can do in a relationship is make ourselves

God over their lives or allow them to become a god in our life. Sometimes what a person needs more than anything is not for us to rescue them but for us to trust God with them. I'm thinking of so many of my friends who have sought to restore broken relationships. It's difficult for us to comprehend what seems like a simple notion, but a heart doesn't have to be wicked to be toxic, and a toxic heart doesn't make a person evil. It simply means they need healing, but we can't provide the kind of healing they need.

What do you do when you aren't so sure there will be glory after you drink from a cup that seems far too bitter to survive? You remember that God has a track record of turning dark times into soil and pain into seed. This book is a testimony, not to my strength, but to my broken surrender. You may be waiting on a harvest for all that you've sown, but you are God's harvest and He won't let you stay in the ground.

FOUR

A WAR OF SEED

"And I will put enmity
Between you and the woman,
And between your seed and her Seed;
He shall bruise your head,
And you shall bruise His heel."

—GENESIS 3:15

My husband and I travel so often that it's hard to remember exactly where we were headed when we recall certain memories. One day we were traveling somewhere to go someplace when our flight was delayed. While we waited to board the plane, we decided to grab something to eat in the food court of the very crowded airport. Since we both wanted something different to eat, we split up and agreed that whoever got their food first would hunt for a table.

I was in line minding my own business, which is my custom, when I noticed a group of men walking nearby. They were dressed in all black, their eyes outlined with heavy dark eyeliner. One of them had an upside-down cross adorning his neck. Another had the same symbol imprinted on his shirt, but with a star placed in a circle above it. I went to high school with kids who went goth over summer break. This was not that.

There was a look and energy to the men that let me know that this wasn't just a costume they put on to walk through the airport, but an ode to a belief that they held near and dear. They were walking through the airport with a menacing look, and then suddenly they were headed my way.

Let me tell you how I turned into an old praying church grandmother standing in that line, waiting for my food. I was pleading the blood of Jesus, rebuking the devil, and manufacturing any kind of heavenly language I could find. I already told y'all I don't watch scary movies, so you already know. I. DON'T. PLAY. WITH. THE. DEVIL. OR. NONE. OF. HIS. FRIENDS! If I didn't already believe that evil existed, I would have become a believer that day. I was relieved to see them walk away when the options for food by our gate failed to meet their criteria.

When I finally made it back to my husband to discuss what I'd just seen, I told him it was my first time being exposed to the blatant worship of Satan. Sure, I've heard about it online or in the news, but I'd never actually seen anything like that with my own eyes. To be honest, I was proud of myself because I looked them right in the face without any sign of fear. It was the first time I felt like my light was truly put to the test, and it had an opportunity to shine brighter than any darkness that stood in my way.

Looking back on that scene, I realize how much easier it is to stand up to a devil you can see than it is to fight the one that hides in plain sight. We see the power of hate, wickedness, and darkness every single day. It's plastered on the news, with stories of senseless violence, acts of terrorism, and schemes rooted in greed. When we're made aware of evil, we demand justice for those who have been affected by it, pray for the victims, and do what we can to make a difference.

I'm constantly praying that I won't become so conditioned to hearing bad news that I become desensitized to the real devastation that a headline has wreaked on the lives of those who've been affected the most. Prayerfully, we will never come to a place where we cease to be grieved by something no matter how normal it has become. Our hearts should break every time we hear of death, injustice, disease, poverty, and so much more. When our hearts no longer break when witnessing human depravity, we've already begun to accept what God wants to reject.

It can seem daunting to always have to be that sensitive and vulnerable to the condition of our brothers and sisters, especially when it feels like we have no power to stop a problem so much bigger than us. This is why having tough and awkward conversations is so important. You alone may not have enough knowledge or power, but coming together to make room for God is all we need.

I'll never forget when COVID-19 hit and our world became more codependent than it has ever been. There was only one clear way to stop the spread of the virus: we all had to agree to wash our hands, wear a mask, and stay six feet apart from each other (social distance). When someone was of the mindset that they were only one person, and that it wouldn't make a difference if they did not follow that protocol, there was a greater case of contagion in the community. On the other hand, when everyone followed the protocol, there was a decrease in the spread, and the hospitals were able to properly treat people without concerns of patient overcrowding.

I believe the cure to what cripples society can be found in its members. And that when we are freed from the bonds that shrink our confidence, creativity, hope, and potential, we are able to create ideas and strategies that revitalize the world we're living in. You may think you're just one person and that you can't make a difference—as long as you believe that, you can guarantee that you won't.

WHAT CAN WE DO?

My hope is to empower a generation of people who believe that if we all do our part, the world will have no choice but to be subdued. Your healing, recovery, and determination to move beyond where you are and lay hold of what God has for you is not just so you can be proud of who you have become. It's even greater than proving other people wrong about what they said about you. God has entrusted you with vision, power, talent, gifts, and anointing so we can wage war against any and every limitation this world has ever seen. What if you came to a place where you didn't just see setbacks, disappointments, and discouragement as facts of life, but rather as a devil hiding in plain sight?

At some point along the way, something changed in me. I came to a place where I realized I wasn't just going to sit back, shake my head, and watch the world dissolve. If I'm in this world, then something or someone will become better because I took up space. I am not neutral. I am utterly convinced that God has given us power meant to be released into the world.

I'm no longer asking God to exclusively grant us wisdom, strategy, and grace for the evil we see. I'm asking God to make me aware of what is in my heart, home, or community that is at war with my ability to partner with God in bringing the world to its greatest potential. I don't know where the devils I can't see are hiding, so I have to be intentional about making sure I'm postured to defeat any negative paradigm or thought that dares to dilute the power God has given me to effect change.

You can't assume this posture and at the same time be married to the idea that you're perfect. Assuming this posture is only possible when you realize your humanity is fragile and that there may be areas of brokenness in you that you have yet to uncover.

When I removed the pressure to be perfect from motivating me, I was able to better acknowledge when I could have done or said something better. This was challenging for me because I felt like my performance reflected my worth.

Your performance does not reflect your worth. The only way that your performance can ever get better is if you live in the consciousness that even being wrong is a blessing because it can help you be better the next time around.

I have learned that the greatest character pursuit one can embark on is maintaining a teachable heart that strives for humility, grace, and understanding. When we make the decision to untether ourselves from what makes us shrink, we can begin reaching for our divine identity—which has power.

Addiction, depression, suicide, abandonment, rejection, low self-esteem, sabotage, and procrastination are not just out to slow you down. Those issues and so many more that I didn't name are waging war on your ability to produce. If we don't see our detrimental patterns as threats to our destiny, we will run the risk of being empty and unfulfilled. Your spirit knows when there is more even when your present is trying to convince you otherwise.

It's so easy to become comfortable living beneath our potential, not stretching for the highest version of who we are. We become complacent because we can still function, but we have two choices. We can choose to function, or we can choose to revolutionize our world.

GOD CREATED US TO PRODUCE

When God was in the garden and He blessed creation, then told them to be fruitful and multiply, I don't think He was just talking about having sex and making babies. I believe that God was preparing humanity to live in a perpetual state of production where we are to take what God has given us, plant it, and allow it to produce over and over again.

When the serpent invaded Eve's realm and convinced her to eat from the tree, he was manipulating God's formula to fit his agenda. The serpent had a plan for the woman to be fruitful and multiply, but this time the fruit wouldn't make the world better. This time the fruit would separate humanity from God's vision.

The moment the woman ate from the tree, the serpent's idea was fruitful. But the moment God cursed the serpent in Genesis 3:15, that fruit was in jeopardy of no longer being able to multiply.

Let me quickly break this down for you. It doesn't matter what seed has been fruitful in your life. Your family may have been producing the type of fruit that has caused dysfunction for generations, but it is never too late to decide that the fruit can no longer multiply with you.

Someone has to make a decision that there is some fruit that cannot remain on your watch. So, girl, grab your journal, and let's make some decisions.

Working It Out

To the best of your ability, draw two trees.

On one tree I want you to write in the characteristics and virtues of your family that you value. Loyalty, kindness, generosity, connection, integrity, and straightforwardness are all things I'd add to my tree.

Now, on the second tree I want you to write down the areas where bitter fruit or no fruit at all has become the norm. You have permission to be completely vulnerable and transparent about this tree. I also think it's worth mentioning that just because there are areas where your family may have harmful patterns, it doesn't mean that your family's worth has been diminished. Of course, the opposite is also true. No matter how well a family has done up until now, that doesn't mean that there isn't room for even more growth. We should all desire to blaze a new trail within our family.

EXAMINE YOUR FRUIT

Jesus gave us insight into the character of God and how He works to bring His creation to its most beautiful existence: "I am the true vine, and My Father is the vinedresser. Every branch in Me that does not bear fruit He takes away; and every branch that bears fruit He prunes, that it may bear more fruit" (John 15:1–2).

This text lets us know that God is looking at the areas of our lives where we are not bearing any fruit or areas that have produced less fruit than what is possible. I don't want the fact that I'm producing on some level to blind me of an area where I could be producing even more fruit.

Also, this process of becoming a fruitful tree doesn't just occur organically. The foundation of why this happened for Jesus was because Jesus was completely surrendered to becoming the most glorified version of himself that He could become. The process of that glorification required that He undergo a process of having His life examined and surveyed.

Allowing the examination of your ways and thoughts to be seen by God is honestly not much different from what we see Adam and Eve doing in the garden.

God was walking in the cool of the garden looking for Adam and Eve when they began to hide. God called out for them, and Adam spoke up, telling God that when they heard God's voice they hid because they were naked. God responded in Genesis 3:11, "Who told you that you were naked? Have you eaten from the tree of which I commanded you that you should not eat?" It seems like such a simple question, but that was the moment when God helped the man and woman realize that He knows when our thoughts and actions are no longer producing the way He intended.

Let's dissect the character of God in this instance. He didn't berate the man or the woman, nor did He shame them. God gave them space to present the truth as they knew it.

I'm reminded of last chapter's compare and replace. The truth as you know it may not be God's truth. That doesn't mean that we should provide the truth that we think God wants to hear. Instead, we should give God the truth we feel in our soul, with the knowledge that our truth is flawed because it doesn't take in the full perspective that only God can see.

God knew in that moment that the man and the woman were bearing fruit, but it wasn't the type of fruit God intended for them.

When you're aligned with who you're supposed to be in God, you have no need to hide your raw, naked vulnerability from Him. We only begin to hide when we no longer trust that we can be accepted in the truth of who we are. That's why I hid. I knew I was hiding too. I just didn't want God to see how badly damaged I was. I wanted to present to God this pure, untouched, perfect version of who I was, and when I thought I'd lost the ability to do that, I didn't want to present anything at all.

I had too much respect for God to show Him just how upset, wounded, and damaged I truly was. I didn't realize that God wasn't asking me to present perfection. He only wanted me to present truth. Perhaps that's where so many religious institutions have gotten it wrong. We spend so much time focusing on the ideal life to present to God that we alienate people who feel they will never meet that mark. Don't fall into the trap of only presenting your good parts to God. You're a person, not a persona. It's much easier to present a persona to God than to present a person, but God doesn't want who you can pretend to be. God wants who you truly are. Away with the personas and the highlight reel that strokes our ego and convinces us that we've made God smile. Instead, we dare to invite God into the ugly truth even if we have to do it trembling in fear. God wants your anger, suspicion, depression, aggression, frustration, bitterness, laziness, procrastination . . . Chiiillle, God wants your truth, whatever it may be! The longer we stay bound, the longer we're rendered ineffective in producing change in this world.

Think about it this way. You're more than just a person on a mission to live a good life. When you wake up in the morning, darkness trembles because the potential of your light is so bright that darkness could lose its power. Heaven knows what's in you, darkness is afraid of it, and for far too long you've not realized how truly powerful you can become. Your power may start as a seed, but that seed has victory over every defeat connected to it.

THE POWER OF THE CURSE

How do I know we have power to defeat the enemy? The Bible tells me so! In Genesis 3:14–15, after the man and woman God created caught God up on their perspective of what occurred in the garden, He responded by introducing a plot twist that took them all by surprise. His response to the mayhem begins in verse 14, where He cursed the serpent to live the rest of his life on his belly. He cursed him more than all the cattle, and every other beast out in the field, and also cursed him to have to eat dust. But it's verse 15, theologically referred to as the Curse, that gave me the revelation I felt every woman should hear.

Get this. God told the serpent that the most damning part of the curse would not be that he would slither around on his stomach or that he would eat dust. What he should *really* be afraid of had to do with how God was going to use enmity between him and the woman.

Out of all the creation God could have chosen to put the serpent at odds with, why did He choose the woman? God could have reasoned that the serpent was already so cunning and had successfully deceived the woman once before and could do it again. I know for sure that, in today's society, we would not have allowed the woman to have a second chance. We would have logically deduced that the woman would be no match for the serpent to face off with again. But not God! God had so much faith that the woman could overcome the serpent that He signed up the woman for a rematch.

Chiiillle, hold my wig while I shout!

If you're like me, you've been wondering why God would keep signing you up for something that you've already failed at before. You don't understand why God would keep blessing you and trusting you with a fresh new start after you've fallen short. I hear God saying, *I have more faith in my creation than my creation has faith in itself.*

I don't care how many losses you have under your belt. Each morning you open your eyes, I want you to start hearing the bell go off because that's God's way of saying He has signed you up again for a rematch.

A rematch at what?

God is giving you another chance to not allow darkness to have the final say. You may have gone to bed depressed, but when the morning comes, you've got another chance to get the help, support, and counseling you need. You may have gone to bed rejected and abandoned, but when you opened your eyelids, God gave you a chance to walk in the knowledge of already being loved and seen by Him.

I know we've grown up thinking that we shouldn't use the word *hate* because it's such a strong word, but there are some things we're going to have to hate if we're going to awaken our greatness. You're going to have to come to a place where you hate everything that is against the manifestation of the divine version of who you are. The word *enmity* means hostility or hate. God says, *I'm going to make the woman hate you because you attempted to keep her from living the life that I predestined for her.* If you're like me, you were admonished growing up not to use the word *hate* because *hate* is a "strong word." Yet *hate* is the word that breaks the tie we have with the habits and choices we know keep us from reaching our destiny. Only when we hate them will we do whatever it takes to break away from them.

I love that God doesn't make the hostility a one-way street. God lets the serpent know that what happened in the garden is just the beginning of the battle, not the end.

Whew! Just typing that blessed me.

I'm imagining myself at thirteen years old rubbing my rounded belly. I was pregnant with my son and shame at the same time. I imagined the serpent was somewhere, pleased with how I stumbled, but God knew that the serpent and I were just getting started.

Okay, so I wasn't actually in the garden facing off with a serpent, but I was facing off with the same spirit that plotted the fall of humanity. I had hostility in my heart, but it was misdirected. I had hostility toward myself for being in the situation in the first place. I didn't know that the misplaced hostility would make me become an enemy to myself. When I finally came to the realization that I couldn't love myself and be hostile toward myself at the same time, I needed a place to properly direct that hostility.

I've met so many women who became hostile toward themselves because of who they were or where they were in life. Hostility is not uncommon to the woman's journey, but that hostility is not being channeled properly. Stop being hostile to your past, body, potential, art, and creativity. Take that hostility and start using it to dismantle the narrative of shame, regret, disgust, depression, and disappointment that plagues far too many of us.

My husband has always said that women have been the most persecuted group on the planet. For me, this scripture affirms my husband's assertion. God trusted the woman with hostility. Not so she could beat herself up, but so she could learn to stand up and become hostile with her true opposition.

To me, it speaks to how God trusts women with power. I grew up in church where it wasn't uncommon to hear about how the devil did this or that. I don't know about you, but I want to flip the script. Little devils and demons somewhere in hell are stressed about what Sarah Jakes Roberts did today. Girl, we are the devil's worst nightmare!

WE ARE AT WAR

This Bible text isn't only about the woman having hostility toward the serpent; it lets us know that the serpent is going to hate the woman. You know why? Because when a woman recognizes who she is, she inspires everyone in her influence to do the same. The most dangerous weapon on the earth isn't made of metal and doesn't require bullets. The most dangerous weapon on the earth is a woman who recognizes that she has been anointed to unleash hostility to her adversary.

Let me tell you a little something about yourself that you may not realize. We are not just learning to navigate our insides for the sake of finally silencing the voices in our head. We are preparing to rise up like an army to make sure that the enmity that God declared in Genesis 3:15 is not a one-way street. I bet you can tell me all the ways it feels like the serpent is hating on you. I wonder if you can tell me how you're making sure the serpent knows you're sending that hate right on back his way.

This is not just a book you're holding. This is me swinging back at the enemy. I stood by, depressed, stressed, discouraged, attacked, and broken for far too long while doing nothing in return. When I finally got to a place of believing that God still had a plan for my life, I took the only tool I had, a laptop, and began declaring to any woman who could hear it that they could come out of darkness too.

Why? Because I wanted nothing more than to swing back at the devil. If the words that are in my heart flow to the paper the way that God has given them to me, I will be preparing you to do the same. I want to challenge you to view everything in your life as more than an opportunity to serve your wants, needs, or desires; view it as an opportunity to push darkness away. We're doing the work here for you to experience supernatural freedom, but it won't stop there.

The purpose of you being delivered from your pain, shame, regret, fear, or depression is not for you to have a happily-ever-after. Your deliverance from everything that has so easily ensnared you is so you can become intentional about loosening the chains from another person's life. I already know for some of you, the moment you picked up this book, random things began distracting you. I'm willing to bet that someone had to go through hell to get it and a second hell to have enough time to finish it, but whatever you've gone through, just know that as you turn every page, you're swinging harder and harder at the serpent's plan.

Here's some serious food for thought.

- How does this new perspective change the way you engage in your world?
- How does it change the way you dream?
- Can you attach the vision for your life to a chain you want to break? (If not, then go back to the drawing board.)
- How are you going to use what God has given you to destroy what has been bound?
- I feel like for some of you the desire to dive into this book, and deeper into relationship with your God-given identity, is already breaking a generational chain off of your life. The question is, what other chain is God calling you to break?

Perhaps you're the first person in your family and world to ever get serious about abandoning religion and pursuing relationship. You may be the only person in your community focused on financial literacy. You're more passionate than anyone you know in areas of mental, emotional, and/or physical health. You desire to see entrepreneurship, education, and corporate experience become the norm in your family. That's no small thing! That's God giving you laser focus to destroy chains.

When my husband and I were dating, I recognized that he had many qualities that would make him a good partner and spouse—but what was most important to me was how God could use our union to break a stronghold off of our lives, our children's lives, and our world.

If you don't leave this book with anything else, my prayer is that you will walk away with the consciousness of seed. In Genesis 3:15, once God established there would be enmity, He took it one step further and defined that the enmity would be between the seed of the woman and the seed of the serpent. I've already detailed for you how the serpent didn't have an obvious plan detectable to Eve. All the serpent had was seed. That seed took root in Eve's life. It changed the way she thought, and then it changed the way she acted. That's why we can leave no room for even the smallest seed of division, confusion, disappointment, or depression. The moment we acknowledge that a seed has been planted that is trying to strip us of our identity, we must take action to uproot it.

We must also recognize that God desires to give us seed. God wants to give us seed that will help us defeat whatever stands in our way. Maybe we're so busy asking God for things that we aren't asking God for seed. Maybe you're reading this book and you've had moments where you felt numb and barren. That emptiness on the inside of you has been calling out for something that would make it go away. You've tried everything you could, but nothing has helped you turn the corner. I feel like God wants you to know that what you call emptiness, He calls soil.

Just as God did in Genesis, when He directed the earth to bring forth fruit and it did, when His will aligns with your hunger, you will bring forth every seed God has placed in you.

Seed is so much bigger than a gift or talent, though it can be that. The seed that God gives you is the part of your identity that looks like God. Maintaining kindness in a cruel world is seed. Being faithful over a craft that infiltrates and changes hearts for the better is seed. Serving is seed. Patience is seed. When the fruit of God's spirit shows up in your life, that is God's seed in you combating the serpent's seed.

Galatians 5:22–23 gives us perspective on the kind of fruit that reflects the spirit of God: "But the fruit of the Spirit is love, joy, peace, longsuffering, kindness, goodness, faithfulness, gentleness, self-control." We have to work our seed until our seed becomes fruit.

FIVE

WORK THE WAIT

And Adam called his wife's name Eve, because she was the mother of all living.

—GENESIS 3:20

As we begin to do the inner work that leads us closer and closer to God's perfect plan for our lives, we can expect to discover purpose and passion that makes us ponder, *Maybe this is why I was born.*

Generally, when we think about who we are, we begin by naming off the titles and roles we possess. I am a wife, mother, daughter, entrepreneur, leader, pastor, and author. Actually, that's not who I am, it's what I do. But it can be exceptionally hard to know the difference.

Answering the question of who you are is impossible without understanding your essence. Ask yourself, *What is my consistent offering to my job, family, friends, and community?*

I am a servant, lover, carrier of joy, motivator, facilitator of environments, listener, and believer. Those qualities make up who I am, but they also show up in each of my roles. And the combination of those qualities gives me distinction regardless of the environment I'm in.

While we do not want to make the mistake of making who we are become synonymous with what we do, we can't ignore what we do altogether. What you do and how you do it should all stem from who you are. My servanthood, love, joy, listening, believing, and facilitation of environments all show up in how I function as a wife, mother, daughter, entrepreneur, leader, pastor, and author.

YOUR HOW IN YOUR NOW

Many of you reading this book aspire to see your life revolutionized from the inside out. Some goals you want to accomplish will be directly related to what you do or what you'd like to do one day, but you aren't exactly sure how to get there.

I feel like this is where Eve landed once the aftermath of what took place in the garden settled in. God expanded her purpose, but God didn't leave a road map behind detailing how to get there.

Is that how you feel? On one hand, you know exactly what you're supposed to do, but you also have no clue how you're supposed to do it. I really believe that, like Eve, your how is buried in your now. Maybe that's not your story, and you feel like knowing what you're supposed to do with your life, but not knowing how you're supposed to do it, would be a welcomed burden. I've got some thoughts that I believe will help you too.

You don't have to know every detail of your purpose or even what your purpose is in order to set your life up *for* purpose. That's part of the reason I want to stress how significant it is for you to come to a place where you trust who you are. Your inability to trust who you are will also show up in what you do. We falsely believe that we'll become confident in who we are when we "arrive," but we fail to realize that confidence is what leads us there in the first place.

If you don't think you are eloquent, intelligent, savvy, or confident enough for the journey ahead of you, it will show up in how you perform. And when your performance doesn't stand out, it leaves very little, if any, room for promotion, connection, and networking. It's a vicious cycle, because from there you won't volunteer to take on new challenges, you won't push yourself beyond what is necessary, and you may even begin to sabotage opportunities because you don't trust yourself to live up to the standard you have in mind.

If your mind is anything like mine, you're wondering how you balance the real feelings of uncertainty when starting in a new field while maintaining who you are. I'm not suggesting you don't get nervous, or that you walk into any room with a false arrogance. What I am saying is that when you walk into the space, you have to make a decision within yourself that no matter what happens, you will not allow the outcome to take away from who you are and all the hard work you've been doing.

This is exactly what I tell myself before I speak. I'm usually super nervous because I want to perform well. I want to meet God's expectations and those of the people in the room. When I live in that nervous space, I talk fast, my words get jumbled, and I lose my train of thought. I end up literally doing the opposite of what I hope to do. When I take a few deep breaths and remind myself that when I am authentically who God has called me to be, so much so that I cannot fail, it eases the tension. I may still have nerves, but I remind my nerves who I am.

When you come to a place where you are confident that your mistakes don't define you, that a person can't outshine you, and that failure is a blessing in disguise, you bring a level of confidence and fearlessness that sets you apart no matter what room you're in. This doesn't mean that you should walk into spaces unprepared and winging it. On the contrary. You have to be even more intentional about doing your homework by understanding your audience and what matters to them. You want to know that you've done everything you know to do when you walk into the room. When you've done your homework, you're less afraid of taking a pop quiz.

Isn't that what scares us from breaking out of our comfort zone in the first place? We don't want to be confronted with a pop quiz that proves we're not as equipped and knowledgeable as we thought we were. You can't avoid failing in life, but you can do everything within your power to prepare.

When faced with failure, you get to choose whether it becomes a lesson or a deterrent to keep you from trying again. I don't know about you, but I've made up in my mind that failure is going to have to work very hard if it's stepping into the ring with my faith.

So you're getting ready to roll up your sleeves and allow the work that's been taking place on the inside to start showing up on the outside. You're ready to start doing the work to build out the full vision God has given you.

Many women I've met have a passion to start a business, serve their community, climb the corporate ladder, write a book, or create a ministry, but they don't feel they have the tools to make that happen. I can't promise you that I can give you all the tools, but I do want to provide you with important insights to help you keep your ambition off pause, begin to overcome obstacles, and pursue these desires.

BE PURPOSEFUL

First things first. You are seed, and you have seed.

You are what God has planted in the earth. Within you He has placed seed that will spring from your life so the earth can be sustained. Have you ever seen an apple seed? It's so small and seemingly inconsequential, but we all know that there is more to that seed than we can see. When given an opportunity to be planted, nurtured, and nourished, that small seed can become a mighty tree.

That's you. You're an apple seed. You're learning the beauty of being planted, nurtured, and nourished so that you provide sustenance to the world.

Purpose is the sustenance you offer to the world. I believe that purpose happens in steps. Sorry, I know you probably wanted me to give you one cure-all sentence, but I'm not so sure it's that simple.

1. **AGREE.** You must come into agreement that your existence is seed. You are not random. How you start is not an indication of how you will finish. Even if your childhood included elements of trauma, it doesn't mean your seed has been damaged. If you're still living, breathing, and reading this book, then God is trying to let you know that there is still somewhere God can place you on this earth that will yield a version of you that looks more and more divine. This isn't even about knowing what you will become; rather it's acknowledging that you're here to become more and more like what God had in mind.

2. **PROTECT.** Because you aren't exactly sure who you are becoming, you must make sure to protect your environment from any

habit, friendship, relationship, or opportunity that could stunt your growth. Let's go back to the apple seed example. Did you know that just because you take the seed of a Granny Smith apple and place it in the ground, that doesn't guarantee it will produce Granny Smith apples? Producing an apple tree takes more than just planting a seed in the ground. Variables, including the soil, pollen, and climate, all play a role in determining what kind of apple the tree will produce. We know that you are seed, but we don't know what kind of tree God is creating. It's not enough for you to be planted. You need people and opportunities in your life that reflect who you're becoming. You are the only person responsible for making sure you are vigilant in protecting the seed you are in God's mind.

3. **NURTURE.** Finally, when your fruit seed begins to take root, you have to consider how you can continue the act of nurturing it. You will know that something is nurturing your seed when it begins to cut through your fears and insecurities and begins to motivate and empower you. This may come from reading a book like you're doing now, hearing a speech, listening to a song, or connecting with someone you know. Make sure you take notice of the moments when you feel someone is nourishing your seed.

Though countless people have asked me, "How do I find my purpose?" realizing that you *have* a purpose is actually better than knowing what your purpose is.

When you don't know what your purpose is, you allow yourself to live randomly while still hoping to one day be awakened to why you are on the earth. When you recognize your life is meant to serve the world, even when you don't know how you will leave your unique distinction, you begin to find purpose in all that you do. Your ultimate purpose may not be evident to you now, but how are you making where you are now purposeful?

Sometimes I go to the grocery store and walk around aimlessly while talking to my mother on the phone. Don't judge me. It's sometimes the closest I can get to a vacation. Other times I have a short window, so when I go into the store, I do so with the intent to not be distracted or delayed.

Are you walking through life like you have no purpose, allowing yourself to become easily distracted? Or are you walking around life confident that you must protect your space and energy so you can recognize your purpose when it comes?

How would you be living if you *knew* you had a purpose versus just wondering what your purpose is? Implement that lifestyle now because it makes you open and available to truly filter through what can live in the realm of your purpose. For instance, some relationships only work because you're both lost and confused about who you are on the earth. You don't have to know every detail of who you are to know that you don't have time for random.

FUEL FOR YOUR PASSION

After God gave the curse in the garden to the woman, her life had a more refined purpose. She no longer had time for random. In Genesis 1, God gave humanity a broad purpose and vision for their existence. After the woman ate from the fruit, her original purpose didn't change, but her route became more nuanced and unique to her experience.

There are some aspects of your purpose that God won't reveal to you until you have the fuel to overcome whatever hell may stand in your way. Sometimes God gives the vision first and then we have to muster up the fuel to get the vision moving. Then other times God gives us the fuel before we receive the vision.

Can you imagine Eve never eating from the fruit, but then God informing her that she would have enmity with the serpent? She would have run out of gas because her fight had no passion behind it. The woman's experience with the serpent gave her the motivation she needed to face off with him.

You may not have your direct orders yet, but I want to challenge you to get in position so that when God throws the ball your way, you'll be ready to take on whatever He is directing you to do.

God gave Eve a word about the role she was to play in helping God establish presence in the earth. Instead of asking God to tell you your purpose, try asking God what role you can play in establishing His presence on the earth.

For me, purpose is an individual assignment reserved for each person to work in tandem with God to bring heaven to Earth. Where are you most passionate about seeing the character of God show up in the earth? Is it for teen moms, the criminal justice system, foster care, church, entertainment? That passion is trying to give you a clue about where you can partner with God.

I mentioned Romans 8:28 earlier: "And we know that all things work together for good to those who love God, to those who are the called according to His purpose." I've challenged myself not to focus on the first part of that sentence so much that I miss the qualifier that comes at the end. What you're going through, God can use to work for you, when you're committed to making sure your life is working toward what God wants. Does that mean you won't experience challenges or heartbreak? Absolutely not. It does mean that there won't be anything you go through that God can't use.

What happened in the garden was not what God wanted, but when God gave the serpent the curse in Genesis 3:15, God gave Eve an opportunity to return to a place of alignment with Him so that His purpose could still be manifested despite the setback.

Can I preach to you for a minute?

It doesn't matter what you've gone through. It doesn't matter how behind you think you are. I don't want you to give up on yourself because you feel like you're too far from any possibility of restoration. God has a promise that good is still possible when you are aligned with Him.

Did you hear me? Good is still possible.

The same God that put Eve back in the game and set her up for victory over what attempted to defeat her is working on your behalf. You may have tried and failed, but at least you know what you're up against when you try again.

You want to talk about all things working together? God's curse gave Eve a more strategic purpose, but the serpent's trick gave her fuel. Genesis 50:20 has to be one of the most quoted verses in church. It speaks to how an enemy can mean something for evil, but God can use it for good. In the scripture, Joseph talked about an evil act by his brothers that God ultimately used to position him for greatness. With the woman in the garden, the serpent meant for Eve to eat from the tree, but God would ultimately use that moment as a catalyst to redeem all of humanity.

I can't just skip past the fact that everything God would use to redeem humanity was in play at the time that God gave the curse. The Bible tells us that God redeemed humanity by partnering with a woman to bring Jesus Christ into the earth. If all God needed was a woman, a serpent, and God's seed, why did we have to wait thousands of years for God to bring Mary into the picture? Because there is a development that can't be rushed that must take place before purpose is fulfilled.

We aren't born with the awareness of our purpose, and even when we discover it, we often have to wait many years to see the value and effectiveness of it. Your purpose is your seed, but you are God's seed, and you must become the tree before you can get the seed. The purpose doesn't grow you up; who you become while waiting is what grows you up. It takes years for an apple seed to become a tree. If it happened overnight, the tree's roots may not be strong enough to withstand the elements and be able to produce.

God, in His infinite wisdom, says there will have to be some seasons when the tree doesn't even know if it's an apple tree; it only knows that it's a tree. There will be other seasons when the tree has to survive the lightning, snow, harsh sun, and rain before it can even bear fruit. Once the tree survives the elements, even if it gets cut down, it's able to grow again because cutting doesn't change your roots. That's why you must be willing to do the work that strengthens your roots.

I love that God doesn't give seed to the woman in the garden at the moment He's made aware of the attack. All He gives her is a promise and time. What she does with that time will determine whether or not the purpose He gave her will come to pass.

DON'T DISCOUNT NOW

By the way, you may or may not have noticed that I have been vacillating between calling Eve by her name versus "woman." That's because up until Genesis 3:20, Eve is only referred to as "the woman." When Adam named her, he gave the woman a unique name given her condition. Adam named the woman Eve, "the mother of all living." I couldn't help but wonder why Adam named this childless woman the mother of all living.

I initially saw it as Adam giving Eve a constant reminder that she was given a responsibility to produce seed. Why would Eve need a reminder that she was called to produce seed? Because as she got further and further away from God's declaration in the garden, she may have run the risk of forgetting that there was a promise connected to her ability to make room for what God said in Genesis 3:15.

I was satisfied living in the concept that Adam named Eve based on where she was headed and not where she was, but then I saw an insight that changed my mind. I believe Adam gave her this name because of who she already was in that moment, not who she could potentially become. She didn't become a mother because Adam wanted to remind her of what to keep reaching for. She was named the mother of all living because of the organic expression of how she cared for all that was living at that time.

When the woman was named Eve, the only form of life that existed was the vegetation and the animals that God had placed in the earth before her. While she may have not been a mother in the traditional sense, she was given the responsibility to use where she was as practice for where she was headed. I doubt very seriously that Eve was as confused by her name as I was. She had no point of reference for motherhood that could make her feel like caring for the animals and vegetation was a demotion. All Eve had was her present circumstance and a calling that extended beyond her.

How often do we discount our now because it doesn't reflect where we've been called? We fail to realize that our now qualifies us for our next. Let's talk about that. Most of us know that Eve eventually gives birth to children and we will dive into that later, but before she gives birth to her own children, she learns to become a mother by nurturing what is around her. This is a valuable lesson worthy of digging into because so many of us think that when we arrive at a certain role or position, then we will innately possess the characteristics, work ethic, and communication skills that will make us successful.

We all remember growing up and critiquing how our parents raised us, resolving, "When I become an adult, I'll never do that!" While many people worked at not being like their parents, others found themselves repeating the very same things they vowed never to do. They didn't realize that there's no magic switch they could flip to help them turn on a different style of parenting.

My husband openly talks about his lifelong desire to be a good father. He is an exceptional father to our children, and I attribute that success to him keeping that desire in the forefront of his mind. It became the guide that determined what he would or would not do. Professional goals require a similar intentional focusing.

A person who aspires to become a CEO one day doesn't become a leader because she's at the helm of a company. A woman becomes a CEO because of how she executed everything that came before opening the business.

When I dropped out of college, I waitressed at a strip club. But my first real job that didn't include dark rooms, loud music, and scantily clad women was as a receptionist for an international aviation company. As a single mother I was so glad to finally have a job that allowed me to have more traditional work hours. I was working as a temporary receptionist with the promise of becoming permanent if I did well. On the organization chart my role was admittedly the lowest on the totem pole. That didn't matter to me; I was so thankful to have the job that I wanted to make sure my presence added impact. I was hungry to establish my professional identity and to release the belief I had in my ability to work in a corporate environment through my work as a receptionist.

I had no team, support staff, office, or even an extension, but you couldn't tell me I wasn't running things. I created and improved systems for maintaining office supplies. I helped the executive team host luncheons and meetings with presentations that kept the clientele's culture in mind. I was the first one there in the morning and one of the last to leave in the evening.

I skipped lunch, opting to eat at my desk instead of leaving the door unmanned. I submitted time sheets and payroll reports from our contractors to my supervisor for review and approval. My numbers were always double-checked, reports alphabetized, and on her desk before she arrived in the office. If I was given a project or task, I turned it around long before it was due. It didn't take very long before my work ethic began to stand out among the team. I wasn't just doing enough to get the job, with plans to relax once the position was secured. There was a standard I set that I knew I could maintain or surpass because it was organic to how I was able to produce in other areas of my life.

Remember, my passion wasn't connected to the position. It was connected to my desire to grow in the environment. In the same way, the position you're in could be the job of your dreams or the practice field of a lifetime, but it is never time wasted.

Fast-forward to more than a decade later—I'm utilizing those same characteristics that allowed me to stand out as a receptionist to lead the businesses I now own. Creating environments, listening intently, and serving with joy play pivotal roles in how we guide the experience and content we curate at Woman Evolve.

Working It Out

Grab your journal and imagine yourself at the height of success. Don't be limited by certain industries, qualifications, or experience. This is your opportunity to dream. Running a fashion house? Heading up a Fortune 500 company? Teaching at a school that considers a student's total well-being? Whatever it is, jot it down. Then think through these two questions.

1. What are the most important character traits you must possess to maximize your dream role?
2. How are those skills showing up where you are now? It's naive to think those skills emerge overnight. They are muscles that must be exercised in your now so they can be strong for your future.

Sara Blakely sold fax machines in the 1990s, but doing so did not come naturally to her. In an interview with *Entrepreneur* magazine, she shared how she was so terrified to approach prospective clients that she would burst into tears and drive around the block to regroup before going inside the building. She could have allowed the fear and anxiety to make her back away from the career altogether, but she had a vision that one day she'd no longer be selling fax machines because she had her own product to sell. She allowed the now she was living in to prepare her for where she was headed. Where did she land? Sara Blakely is the founder of Spanx, which I'm almost certain is some kind of manna from heaven.

Would she understand consumers, sales, relationships, and presentations the way she does now had it not been for her start selling fax machines? Probably not. The only connection I can see between shapewear and fax machines is Sara Blakely.

Where you are right now may not be connected to where you will land, but where you are right now will serve you when you get to where you're headed.

While you're exercising the muscles you'll need for the journey ahead of you, make sure you don't lose what makes you unique. When I think of how successful women are depicted in entertainment, they're generally very different from how I perceive myself. They're direct, sharp, quick on their feet, and intuitive.

My natural leadership style is much different. I'm a "feeler." I lead with my heart, and I trust my gut. I like to make sure my team is doing well on the inside. I've been hurt by words in the past, so I try to be conscious of saying things in a way that teaches but doesn't wound. I haven't had many examples of this type of leadership style, and when I began working with business partners and building the infrastructure for the Woman Evolve movement, I wondered if I was too soft.

I tried for about twelve hours to put on my best Miranda Priestly impression, and it just didn't work. I decided to ditch the act and trust that my authenticity would be enough, no matter where it showed up. There is a difference between organic growth and simulated change. When you grow, there may be parts of you that begin to take on a new form. Never apologize for that. When you force yourself to fit a mold created by people who don't value your authenticity, you cheat on yourself and become faithful to an image you can't maintain.

This is exactly what happened to Bozoma Saint John early in her career. A colleague suggested that she never wear red nail polish or red lipstick in the workplace. She told Bozoma it would be too bold of a message to send and she wouldn't be taken seriously. She took the advice but eventually abandoned it. "It's not natural to me. It would make me unproductive in what I do because I would be so focused on being quiet that I can't really show up."[1]

Bozoma is currently the chief marketing officer for Netflix and has proven consistent upward mobility throughout her impressive career, all while keeping her bold presentation intact. "By bringing your whole self to work you can bring full ideas and the wholeness of you," said Saint John. "You are the only you, so why not bring that?"[2]

When God gives you an opportunity, He isn't expecting you to become someone else to fulfill it. He created that opportunity for a specific, authentic version of you. The counterfeit version of you may squeeze into that space, but eventually you will have to choose to be who you truly are or risk not being able to experience the fullness of why God has placed you there.

Everyone has tried to force a puzzle piece to fit in a space that it's not made for. You cram it in there and try to ignore the fact that your thumb almost went numb trying to smash it in. You don't acknowledge that the lines aren't quite adding up. You're so ready to move on to the next part of the puzzle that you don't think that one little piece will matter. Then what happens? You can't even enjoy the rest of the puzzle because you see that one little piece bulging out from what was supposed to be a beautiful picture.

Moral of the story? Don't be that awkward puzzle piece, sis.

SIX

IT'LL NEVER ADD UP

But He said to them, "You give them something to eat."
And they said, "We have no more than five loaves and
two fish, unless we go and buy food for all these people."

—LUKE 9:13

What do you think is the most important miracle Jesus performed? I already know somebody just thought *turning water into wine* in their head. Stay focused, my friend, I personally don't think that's it. Jesus performed so many miracles that never made it into the Bible, but of the ones we're told about, one sticks out in my mind.

In all honesty, I don't think this miracle was necessary. Throughout the Gospels we see Jesus perform wonders that change people's lives. A lame man walks. A dead girl comes back to life. A blind man sees. A woman is healed from an incurable flow of blood. Even the water to wine miracle—which was what kickstarted Jesus' public ministry.

The miracle that stands out in my mind seems somewhat unnecessary given there was another alternative. Here's the backstory.

Jesus was preaching to the multitude—which simply means a lot of people. The Bible tells us that there were about five thousand men in attendance. Most theologians believe the number was likely double that because the patriarchal systems at that time alienated women and children and did not include them in the official count.

As the daytime drifted to evening, the disciples told Jesus to send everyone away so they could go into town to get something to eat. This doesn't seem like an unreasonable request, given the people had the ability to pay for their food and there was no disability or danger prohibiting them from returning to their norm. Jesus gave His disciples a shocking response. He directed the disciples *not* to send the people away but instead said to them, "You give them something to eat."

The disciples responded, "We have no more than five loaves and two fish, unless we go and buy food for all these people" (Luke 9:13).

This is where your girl got stuck.

The disciples had come up with a reasonable solution for the hunger of the crowd. The solution would not create any undue stress on anyone involved, yet Jesus insisted they look beyond what was reasonable and discover how they could be obedient to the command He gave them. (Pivotal shifts don't occur without unreasonable requests, but that's another book for another time.)

In John's gospel we learn that a young boy in the crowd had the five loaves of bread and two small fish. It certainly wasn't enough to feed five-thousand-plus people, but the disciples offered it as a possible solution anyway (John 6:3–13).

I've always thought this text about an unnecessary miracle had so many layers to it. And I've heard messages preached in church with about a thousand different applications. But for our purposes, there are a few perspectives I feel will serve you in unfolding this next dimension of who you are becoming.

THE BOY: UNCOMFORTABLE VULNERABILITY

Can you imagine being the young child in this story? Don't let the fact that you know the ending keep you from imagining what it was like to be the boy in the moment when he was asked to hand over his lunch. In my mind I see a young boy, maybe nine years old or so, handing over a basket of his food to adults scrambling to figure out the best way to solve the hunger of the huge crowd.

The boy doesn't have a food supply shortage, and could have kept his lunch to himself, but something in him realized the food may have a greater impact if he partnered with the disciples than it would have if he kept it to himself. Still, do you know how much trust it takes to hand over what you have to someone else?

I know so many of you do. I think that handing it over makes it sound like you're in the power position, so I'd like to introduce another word I know will invoke an uncomfortable vulnerability. I honestly believe you can't even expect a miracle if you're not willing to live in a space of uncomfortable vulnerability.

Are you ready for the word? *Surrender.* The boy surrenders what he has to another person.

I want to stress the receiver of his lunch as another person. It's so much easier to surrender when we feel we're giving it directly to God, but what do you do when surrendering to God's will means you must take what you have and trust it to another person? It's not like the little boy was handing it over to Jesus. He was handing it over to one of the many men who were *around* Jesus. Yet he still chose to trust someone he didn't know well with what he had. I guess this is why the Bible tells us that unless we are willing to become like children, we cannot enter the kingdom of heaven.

Only a child would turn over the little he had to a stranger who was trying to feed that many people. I can tell you right now that as an adult I would have had some questions. I would have tried to be polite and suppress my discomfort, but I don't just let people walk away with food I'm planning to eat. At least not without some serious interrogation. Girl, if my husband took my dinner plate away from me at the house, I would probably hit the roof, so a stranger would not stand a chance. This boy represents a beautiful vulnerability that I'm challenged to strive for each and every day. I admire how he was able to offer and trust what little he had to another person.

We've made it a habit to be completely honest in this book, so let's not stop now.

Have you ever felt like you had only a little to give but had to trust someone with it anyway? You only have a little forgiveness. You only have a little faith. You only have a little strategy. You only have a little trust. You only have a little talent. You only have a little space in your life. You see, when you feel like you have an abundance, giving it away is easy, but when you have only a little, it's not so easy to give it away.

Giving your little is easier when the giving is your idea, but what do you do when giving your little requires you to surrender to a business partner's, lover's, parent's, or friend's plan, thoughts, or ideas? I don't think there's any nakedness like the one that comes when life makes you vulnerable to the actions of another person. Yet because we were created to exist dependent on one another, there will be moments when you can't move forward unless you're willing to give your little to someone else. The boy is about to learn the value and cost of partnership.

In business, partnerships are successful when each party has something to lose. On the other hand, partnership without vulnerability can't produce success. Vulnerability is the act of letting someone else see your "little" that doesn't seem like enough, and then trusting that little bit to them. When the right person sees it, they will strategize with you on how to increase it. But too often the wrong person sees it before the right person does. That experience teaches us to never show our little again.

This would be perfectly fine if we weren't on a mission to continue to increase and flourish. But because we are, there comes a moment when the only way that we can find a way forward is if we're willing to partner with someone who proves themselves worthy of having access to our little.

My ability to move forward has not been devoid of uncomfortable vulnerability. I've experienced nerves and anxiety while revealing my shortcomings to another person or entity with the hope that partnering with them would conceal the areas of my deficiency.

In a business relationship this type of partnership is commonly referred to as a merger. It's when two companies merge together to combine their strengths and overcome their obstacles. I experienced this for the first time in 2018. My social media presence was growing, but my ability to truly serve the people who were being transformed by my messages was limited to the internet. That's when I knew I needed to host a conference that would allow me to serve God in supporting their transformation.

We had a little less than two thousand women coming to Denver, Colorado, to participate in an event. I had at least ten times that number of women write telling me they couldn't leave their families, were afraid of flying, or wished I could come to their cities instead.

I decided to test the theory and truncated our two-day conference experience into nightly events around the country. I had the vision, but I didn't actually have the staff, knowledge, experience, or know-how to pull it off. I partnered with a company that could make up for the areas where I had too little.

Sometimes we think we need to put our vision on pause until we can hire the team who can manifest it, not realizing that manifestation may come through partnership. When you have a history of having to get things done on your own, you become conditioned to believing that's the only way you'll ever get anything done. That's simply not true, and until you abandon that notion, you may stay limited in how you're able to get the greatest impact. No one has ever built anything alone. Even Jesus had disciples who helped him fulfill His mission on the earth. There will come a point when you must be willing to let someone into the parts of your life that are not developed so you can experience increase.

That sounds so cute and practical for business, but, honey, believe me, it's not nearly as easy when you're in a relationship. Whether it's professional, friendly, marital, or familial, what determines whether or not the partnership will withstand the test of time is not how well we function in our strength, but how we handle inevitable moments of vulnerability. How do you come to a place where you're able to share yourself without fear of rejection? That can only occur when you've learned to no longer reject yourself. You can't expect another person to do for you what you have been unable to do yourself.

There is likely nothing that produces more vulnerability than giving someone permission to investigate how you choose to spend money. Chiiillle, you talking about more fireworks than the Fourth of July! A 2017 study by Ramsey Solutions (The State of Finances in the American Household) revealed that disagreements about money were the second leading cause of divorce—infidelity was number one. If this statistic is true, I think it has less to do with how we choose to spend money and more to do with what spending reveals about the priorities of the person in the marriage.

———

Letting someone see into the inner workings of your mind, value system, and life is one of the scariest things you can do. This doesn't just apply to finances or marriages either. Letting someone in is what makes being in any relationship hard.

It's easy to celebrate my wins, but can you help me discover my wounds? I read a poem once that went, "I want you to love me the way that I would love me if I were you." Exposing yourself to receive someone else's love is not much different from the little boy offering his lunch to the disciples with no idea what would happen next. I believe a few contributors made it easier for him to turn his lunch over, which I think will also make it easier when you turn your little over to someone else.

Know Where You Are

The boy understood where he was. You've got to know where you are in life when you're giving your little away. Giving yourself away is not something you do when you're lost and confused because you could be giving yourself away to someone just as lost and confused as you are. The lad and the disciples made a mutual sacrifice to be where they were. They weren't in a convenient location hearing Jesus, but rather pushed far away from the town in the pursuit of receiving a word. He didn't have to worry about whether or not they'd take advantage of him or rob him of his lunch because the environment of integrity that brought them together would reveal any wrong before it came to fruition. Who would dare steal in front of Jesus and think they could get away with it?

That's going to help someone who may be afraid that someone will take advantage of them.

Now, it is true, just because you operate in integrity doesn't always mean the person you surrender to is. You can complete all the proper due diligence and feel confident the person's consistency allows you to move forward, yet there is still a chance that something *could* happen. I hope, though, you'll find peace in knowing that God judges each of us based on the character of our hearts. Your pure intentions cannot be contaminated by someone's ill intent unless you let that happen. What's done in the dark will come to light.

Also, because the disciples and the boy were willing to inconvenience themselves to be in the presence of Jesus, they were willing to surrender what little they had so they could experience more. When you work with someone who understands the cost of surrendering to gain more, they treat what you give them with care. They know it's not easy, so they don't take your investment lightly.

Know Who You're With

This brings me to my next point. The boy knew who the disciples were. He didn't just give his lunch away to a random group of men. He gave his lunch away to men who were coming up with a plan. A partner may not bring everything you need to the table, but they will attempt to take what they have and what you have and actively plan how you could become better together. There's nothing like a woman and man with a plan. But here's the deal. If you're going to hijack my plan, you better have a better plan.

One of the greatest barriers my husband had to work through with me when we got married was the faith I put in my own plan.

If I had an idea, I executed it. By the time we got married, I already had a history of devising good plans. I divorced, moved home, saved my money, purchased a house, built a website for blogging, built the blog audience, landed a book deal, and toured the country promoting the book, all while maintaining my full-time job, raising my children, and dating him.

When we got married, I wasn't used to putting my plans on hold to run them by another person. After a couple of years of conversations, I realized that my husband wasn't frustrated that I was doing things without his permission, or because he didn't have faith in my decisions. My husband was frustrated because he believed that together we could make a *better* plan. Girl, I tried incorporating him a few times, and I hated to admit it at first, but my plans were getting better and better with his input.

Surrendering your plan so it can be expanded does not mean your original plan was bound to fail. It means that you value the wisdom of another person and don't want to miss out on an opportunity to turn your good to great. For instance, with the help and insight of another person, you can make a more informed decision about what you're supposed to do next.

One of the things I respect about the company I partnered with for the tour is that even on our initial call they weren't just surveying what I wanted. I could tell they were devising a plan. You receive a certain energy from someone who looks at your little and sees potential. As a parent, my job is to look at where my children have a little to work with and help them increase that little or navigate the world with the little they have. Whether you're considering a potential business partner or navigating a relationship, it will not be successful unless you expose your vulnerabilities. Do not, however, expose your vulnerabilities until you're sure you're exposing them to someone who honors what you're offering, someone who won't violate it with greed, jealousy, or envy.

Know What You Have

The last thing I want to share about the boy with the lunch is that he had an awareness of what he was carrying. What he had may not have been enough to feed the five-thousand-plus people, but it was more than enough for him.

Don't ever let someone make you feel so uncomfortable with your little in comparison to their ability that you cease to remember that your little is more than enough for you.

Girl, you know that just set you free. Read that last sentence until the revelation makes you get up and run a victory lap around the room!

I need you to make up your mind that you will not allow another person to come into your life and shame you or discredit what you're doing just because they think it could be bigger or better. If the business never grew, if the insecurity never went away, if your little stayed little forever, remember that your little survived hell and high water. Your little brought you this far. Your little is valuable in the sight of God. When that little becomes valuable to you, you will demand that anyone who comes into your life must also recognize the beauty in your little.

THE DISCIPLES: UNDERRESOURCED

Now that we've taken a moment to acknowledge the challenge the young boy overcame in order to become vulnerable enough to offer his little, we need to talk about the disciples. I'm sure when they suggested the boy's lunch as a possible option to feed five thousand men plus women and children that even *they* knew it was a total reach. To put it plainly, the disciples were underresourced for the mission at hand.

Can you imagine walking with Jesus and watching Him perform miracle after miracle for other people, yet when it's time for another miracle to be performed, He doesn't count on what He can do, but rather challenges you to see what you can do?

The exchange between the disciples and Jesus highlights a perspective that Jesus had of the disciples that they didn't have of themselves. Jesus' mission was not only to redeem humanity but also to raise up individuals who could continue to spread awareness of humanity's ability to rise above fear, anxiety, insecurity, shame, pride, ego, and all the other bitter fruit that the serpent planted in the garden.

The disciples were content in following Jesus, but Jesus wanted them to come to a place where they recognized they had access to the power working within Him. This is a hard concept to grasp when you've only ever seen yourself through the lens of your ability. Every now and then there comes a moment when you are placed in a position that lays such a high demand on you that it makes you begin to wonder if God is trying to tell you something about yourself that you don't quite know.

You know how we sometimes reject opportunities because we feel unqualified or inadequate to fulfill them? That's got to stop, friend. Instead of thinking about all the reasons you shouldn't be in the circumstance, what would happen if you took a moment and just asked yourself what you could do to become more confident instead of going back to the place of comfort?

This isn't all of you reading this book, but someone reading this book would have failed this test Jesus gave the disciples. I can see the teeth-sucking, lip-smacking, head-scratching, confused look on your face right now—"Man, Jesus is tripping! He's the one who does the miracles. Why are we trying to feed all these folks anyway when they can walk themselves right back down to the city and feed themselves? I quit!"

I don't know if I would've straight up quit, but I definitely would've been giving an ever-so-slight side-eye.

Whether you're shaking your head in agreement or disapproval at that reaction, I think you should consider something. Has there ever been a moment in your life when you were placed in a position to do something that seemed bigger than you, and instead of trusting that you could learn as you go, you decided to shrink back to what you know? I feel like I've seen this play out in many different ways in my personal circle.

I had an offer to participate on a speaking panel, but I didn't feel educated enough, so I declined the opportunity. I've had friends back out of relationships that were making demands on their need to communicate instead of them shutting down as they usually did. I've known business colleagues who had ideas but couldn't obtain the resources to make them a reality.

These moments would've been so much easier to walk away from if they hadn't been brought into our lives by divine confluences. We don't walk away from what God tells us to do and find peace anywhere else. I've learned in my life that avoiding the hard things God asks of me haunts me until I decide to do them.

Actually, because you're reading this book, you no longer have any other option than to put on your big-girl panties and figure out how to overcome the obstacle that's standing in your way. That is, if you want to live with any real peace.

And just in case a wall of fear is trying to invade your mind right now with thoughts that you shrank back the time before and have missed any chance to ever do it again the right way, you should know that you're not the same person you were in that previous situation. The you that you were before may have allowed fear to control her destiny, but that version of you is no longer driving the car. You're coming into the awareness of your fullness. You're coming into the acknowledgment of your ability to no longer face things alone. You're becoming exactly who God has in mind, and God is going to give you the chance to let this version of you show up in an opportunity that reflects your growth. Let's prepare you for that moment.

Feeling Not Enough

I've heard this Proverb spoken over and over again: Your gift will make room for you and bring you before great men (see 18:16). This sounds good in theory, but when you aren't sure about the value of your gift in the face of great men, it can be unnerving. Sometimes we have the faith to exercise our gift, but we haven't learned to trust its value fully. Especially when it's being evaluated by great men.

When your faith brings you into a situation that feels greater than you, it can be overwhelming. When you feel like there's a possibility you are not educated, experienced, connected, exposed, or polished enough, you must recognize that all those moments come down to not feeling like you have the proper resources.

Gaining wisdom and education so you can become well versed for your present circumstance does not mean you are no longer being authentic. Being authentic doesn't mean you'll never grow and change. Authenticity is taking what you've learned and applying it in a way that is unique to how you process, communicate, and create. My grandmother always said, "Life is a classroom, and we're all students." In other words, we are constantly learning and harnessing what we've learned for the road ahead of us. Who you are authentically at twenty-one is different from who you are authentically at forty-one. The goal is to be true to who you are and where you are and not force yourself to fit into shoes you've outgrown.

I don't think there's a community more affected by being under-resourced than educators in underserved communities. This was highlighted during the COVID-19 pandemic. Due to the ban on large gatherings, students were relegated to home education. For most families, making the transition was challenging. Education now depended heavily on technology and parental oversight. There was a glaring issue, however, that needed to be addressed. In under-served communities, where laptops, computers, tablets, and internet services are not as prevalent, the ability to move education exclusively online was nearly impossible. Proper funding for electronic devices and training the students to utilize those devices was an even greater challenge.

This highlighted an issue that educators have been grappling with for years. Being underresourced in an ever-changing world risks leaving a generation of students ill-equipped to maximize their potential.

In response to this dilemma, many teachers moved to districts where funding was more readily available. But other teachers chose to find creative ways to overcome being underresourced. By partnering with parents, organizations, and local colleges, teachers found ways to get students the care they needed so they could reach the benchmarks to prepare them to establish successful career paths. By employing unconventional methods, they were able to overcome their underresourcing.

Working It Out ━━━━━━━━━━━━━━

Let's take a page from those educators' books and apply it to your life. And speaking of pages, yes, get your journal.

1. Where do you feel underresourced?

    I've found that we often stop at feeling overwhelmed, but when we're more specific, we can create a plan. Instead of using blanket thoughts and statements like "I don't have what it takes," try to get specific about where and what you lack for a specific task. Underresourcing can be in any area. In a corporate setting you may feel like you're not qualified for the role or promotion that you'd like. As a student, you may feel like you don't have the resources to dedicate the time you need to your studies. Mothers may feel ill-equipped to raise emotionally healthy children. Even in adult relationships, you may feel like you don't have the communication or emotional skills to present the best version of yourself.

    Once you've identified the area where you feel like you don't have what it takes, consider what the outcome would be if you were sufficiently resourced. The disciples in this story were underresourced for the task at hand; however, they had knowledge of what they were up against. How can you slay a giant you won't even look at?

2. Is there another way?

    I believe the most admirable thing the disciples did after taking into consideration what they were up against was that they then began looking for unconventional methods of accomplishing their goal. Sometimes we think there is only one way for us to overcome what we lack. If we don't have the degree, we lock ourselves out completely. If we don't have the experience, we take the desire off the table. What if you're so restricted to the one way things have to be done that you miss out on the unconventional miracle that God already has in your midst? The disciples could have been married to the notion that the only way to feed the multitudes was to send them back to town, but had they been married to that formula, they would have missed their miracle.

What does it mean to begin looking at unconventional methods? It means that we have to be willing to ask God if there's something already available that could assist us in becoming better prepared. Take inventory of what you do have instead of lamenting over what you don't have. I don't know your unique circumstances, but here are a few tips that have helped me.

- **BORROW OTHER PEOPLE'S KNOWLEDGE.** You may not have the background for the present you're standing in, but someone does. Don't be afraid to seek out advice and/or relationships with people who are miles ahead of you on a similar path. You don't even have to know a person to borrow their knowledge. By reading books, watching interviews, listening to podcasts, and following their social media, you are allowed access to how a person thinks. If you're fortunate enough to have access to them, then be intentional about what you want to learn so they can be intentional about what they give you.

- **BE UNCONVENTIONAL.** Okay, so I didn't finish college. I can't tell you how many times I wish I would have paid more attention in a business management or accounting class. One day I decided I was going to go back to school online so I could begin to really soak in the information I needed. I started looking at the time commitment it would require, and your girl got nervous. It dawned on me that I really just wanted the information I needed and not the full college experience. I started looking up the textbooks for business management classes, ordered them online, and began teaching myself principles in business management. While I may not have had the full experience of my college-educated colleagues, I was able to establish a firm enough foundation to evaluate the best way for me to progress in my respective companies.

- **ASK QUESTIONS.** I haven't always wanted to make my ignorance evident because I didn't want anyone to know how ill-equipped I felt. Well, I learned to stop doing that when I began losing money. Ask your questions. You may have to allow your pride to take a bruising for your knowledge to be increased. Perhaps it's not in a room where everyone can hear it, but make sure to jot down questions as they come up and then speak with a peer or superior at their earliest convenience to get answers to those questions. I consider myself a slow processor, so sometimes I have to ask random questions to paint the full picture in my head. When the picture is painted, though, I'm able to offer valuable insight or ask questions the team hasn't considered. So in honor of great teachers everywhere, make a point to remember one of my educator's favorite sayings: "There's no such thing as a stupid question."

- **GET HELP.** When the disciples finally had even the smallest possibility of a solution, it came from a little boy with a lunch sack. Can you see a bunch of grown men having to humble themselves to ask a little boy for his lunch? At that point there was no room for pride or ego. If you feel underresourced, specifically when it comes to how you're able to relate and connect with people, I want you to get help. Consider joining a support group, getting therapy, or letting someone into your dilemma. You may be in a unique situation that no one in your circle understands. That doesn't mean that someone isn't willing to try to understand. They may not be able to fix your problem, but at least you won't be standing in your problem alone.

- **BE PATIENT.** Never forget that the disciples didn't just decide that they were going to try to feed five thousand people on their own. Jesus gave them a command to feed the people. Not everything God has for you will come easily, but if God has asked you to do it, then He has provision for you to be able to accomplish what He said. In my darkest moments, when I've felt in over my head pursuing what God has requested of me, I've had to remind myself that the pressure isn't mine alone. When we can't see our way through, sometimes being divinely aligned means the best thing we can do is to ask God for patience while *He* reveals our next move.

JESUS: THE MULTIPLIER

The boy, the disciples, the crowd, and Jesus. There are four characters in this story but one reason they've all been brought together. As I mentioned earlier, Jesus is raising up a generation to take his work and go throughout all the earth. He plans to multiply who He is in the earth. I believe this is one of the most important miracles in the Bible because it speaks to God's desire for us to understand multiplication. I know this chapter took us a little bit away from Eve, but in Genesis, God said to be fruitful and multiply. He never said to be fruitful and add. When God does math, it never adds up because it's always about multiplication. The disciples didn't realize that when they were telling Jesus what they had in the boy's lunch, the "little" they actually had was every single thing they needed.

They looked at what they had, and it didn't add up, but when Jesus looked at what they had, He knew they had enough for it to be multiplied. You don't have to have all the right words. You don't need the degrees from the fancy institutions. You don't have to have a pristine family or a white-picket-fence childhood. The only thing you need is something for God to multiply.

Can you imagine the impact teachers have had on the children in underserved communities? Their commitment to sticking with them even when they didn't have everything they needed doesn't just give them a slightly greater chance at being successful—it multiplies the odds.

We know how this miracle ends. Jesus takes the boy's little, the disciple's effort, and His anointing, and a miracle takes place. That's the sweet spot for us as believers. It's not when we're operating in our own strength and wisdom. It's when we come to a place where we combine our uncomfortable vulnerability with our under-resourced effort and lay it at Jesus' feet.

Never forget that God sees what you can't see. He knows the road ahead of you and the world around you. When you give Him something to work with, He gives you something worth the wait. I don't think there's anything that makes us more fragile than taking the most intimate pieces of our journey and turning them over to another. Thank you for allowing this chapter access to your little. I don't take it lightly, and I want to make sure we seal your vulnerability with God's presence. I want to pray over your little.

Heavenly Father, there is truly no one who understands humanity and divinity the way You do. You understand how fragile we feel in this scary world. You know where our fresh wounds are and the places we're hiding scars. Father, I ask that You give every woman reading this book the strength to open herself to You. Open her eyes to how You see her greatness and her sorrow. Grant her courage to stand up in the area where she's tempted to fall. Attract to her teachers, friends, community, and love that force her to raise her head and trust again. Help her to be comfortable in her own skin so the best of her can be multiplied for Your glory. Amen.

SEVEN

GOOD GOES HARD

Then the man said, "The woman whom You gave to be
with me, she gave me of the tree, and I ate."

—GENESIS 3:12

I've got to be honest with you. When God challenged my heart toward Eve, it shifted the way I related to Adam. At first, I felt bad for the guy. I mean, Adam was out there minding his own business, doing what he's supposed to do, when Eve comes over and sets him up for failure.

All that changed when I started relating to Eve. Through that lens of compassion, I saw Adam's response to God regarding what occurred in the garden as throwing Eve under the bus. "The woman whom You gave to be with me, she gave me of the tree, and I ate" (Genesis 3:12). My allegiance to Eve has forced me to consider a new plan when I make it to heaven. I need to do what any good friend would do—confront her friend's partner about him trying to make her look bad in front of the guy in charge. I have it all planned out in my head.

SCENE 1

SJR ENTERS PEARLY GATES OF HEAVEN AND HEADS TOWARD GOLD BOULEVARD

Angelic music begins to play. SJR looks around her in wonder, then spots Adam at a worship service. SJR walks with passion toward Adam.

SJR clears throat and begins to whisper.

SJR: Excuse me . . . 'scuse me . . . You don't know me, but I'm from Earth. I did time from 1988 to 2088. I've been meaning to talk to you about what happened in the garden because it's been upsetting me and my homegirls. Why didn't you do a better job at trying to protect Eve?

SJR's voice begins to rise.

SJR: Like, when you first saw her in the garden, you was all like, "Flesh of my flesh, bone of my bone. She shall be called woman."

SJR's voice now at full yell.

SJR: When you first met her, you were all like, "WWWOOOOO-man," but when she messed up and the big man found out, what did you tell him?

SJR head tilt, lips poked, and dramatic pause.

SJR: All of a sudden, she's "the woman You gave . . ."

SJR is escorted out of heaven by Gabriel and Michael.

END SCENE 1

After playing out that scene with a few reruns, I knew I needed to go back to the text to reconcile my feelings toward Adam. Can you blame me? My loyalty has limits, and I'm not going to hell or jail for nobody! Also, if you're taking notes, you need to know that you can't be petty in heaven. So if you have "aught" in your heart toward someone, you'd better find a way to get that resolved before you get to those pearly gates.

I began the hard work. I knew I had to be willing to see things from his perspective and not through the lens of my newfound affinity for Eve. I closed my eyes, went back to the garden, and imagined being Adam before Eve.

THE FIRST MAN, ADAM

The lone human in a buzzing world of animals, birds, rivers, mountains, and sea stands he. Utilizing his creativity to give unique names to every creature, he takes in the good that is God's gift to him. The first to observe the undisturbed, intricate detail God has placed into manufacturing his home, Adam sees the earth the way it was meant to be. Loneliness is not even a worry or concern, yet God knows one day it will emerge. So into a slumber Adam is placed while the finishing touches to the earth are traced.

Until this moment no species that looks like him has been in his view, and then, with the fluttering of his eyes, Eve comes into view.

Imagine the joy and elation he possesses in finally seeing a creature that looks like him. At the time that God says it's not good for man to live alone, man wasn't requesting a friend or a counterpart. God answered his prayers before he could even pray them. Then Adam worshipped God for knowing him better than he even knew himself.

He gets to live in the beauty of that blessing for only a brief time because, well, you know . . . he shares the world with the woman, and they are surrounded by nothing but goodness, beauty, and grace. Then suddenly it all changes. What happens in the garden does not just result in the fall of humanity. For Adam it represented a shift in maintaining trust when something that God gives you goes from good to hard.

A CURSE OR A BLESSING?

Rehearsing that visual was when the ice melted from my heart and I was able to fully relate to what it must have been like to be Adam.

We have several moments of biblical precedent inviting us on a journey of observing what happens when something that starts off as a good thing becomes challenging. Like when Joseph was placed in prison after already being sold by his brothers or when the children of Israel began rebelling against Moses or when Jesus was in the garden praying until drops of blood fell from His head. If you've ever experienced such a moment, then you know that the first thing we begin doing is wondering if it was God in the first place.

We talk so much about the euphoria and peace that come when we're in God's will, but I would not be responsible if I did not prepare you for the moments when good goes hard. You're going to make some decisions, and when you make those decisions, there are going to be some moments when you know you're in God's will.

But sometimes you are also so tired and weary that you aren't sure whether or not you want to stay in God's will.

It's like when a woman makes the decision to be celibate, but then dating becomes a gazillion times harder. Or when you choose to quit the addiction, then realize you won't be able to hang out with your friends without being tempted. You choose to save money, but then you're no longer living the lifestyle you've become accustomed to. You thank God for the children, but the children are driving you crazy. The examples are countless, but the feelings are similar. Good doesn't always equal easy, and easy doesn't always mean that it's good.

Now that we've established the likelihood of having a tough time even when you're doing the right thing, I know what you want to ask: How should I respond when what started off as good becomes hard?

I'm glad you asked! Hopefully you're already beginning to receive some comfort in knowing that you don't have to experience guilt for being overwhelmed or confused about how you feel toward what you know is a blessing. I'm also praying that this serves as a sort of preparation for women venturing out of their comfort zone. I need you to remember that just because something gets hard doesn't mean it's not of God.

Becoming the most divine version of who you are doesn't mean that you'll avoid challenges or difficulties. I know this because I've studied the life of Jesus and it was not all smooth sailing for Him. I know you've had this thought, too, but I'm wondering if you're really okay with this truth.

I think most of us subconsciously believe that surrendering our comfort and pursuing a life that allows God to lead us and guide us should guarantee peace, joy, loyalty, health, provision, and protection. We live with this in our subconscious, and when things happen that are in direct opposition to that belief, we become frustrated and hurt because we thought that our sacrifice would result in perpetual satisfaction. Remember how I told you about God being able to work out all things for our good? Well, in the process of God working, we sometimes don't have a clue what's going on. Not only do we not have a clue, but we often begin to resent that we even trusted God in the first place.

Can we be real? If you were Adam, wouldn't you have wondered whether you were better off by yourself? When God brings a person or opportunity into your life and you no longer feel as blessed as you did when you first met them or received it, I think you have to ask yourself, *Did the blessing change, or did I change?*

There are so many definitions of blessings, but for the sake of this context, I'd like to define a blessing as God allowing His resources to become our own.

Everything that makes our world function began as an idea in God's mind that He extended to Earth. Whether He gave humanity the idea and then facilitated the moments that would bring it to life, or He set it in motion at the beginning of time, blessing is just what God does. That's why every morning I wake up is another blessing. In the beginning, God breathed His breath into humanity. So each morning when I wake up, I'm able to say, "Thank you, God, for allowing me to borrow Your breath today."

Meditation is so powerful because it forces us to take intentional breaths. When we breathe intentionally, we're able to still our mind and bring peace to our spirit. The same thing happens when we're worshipping, praying, or in a service. Why is that? Because when we meditate, we're awakened to the power of our own breathing. That power has a source. Take an intentional deep breath. You just breathed in a blessing.

Sometimes I get so caught up in my tasks and list of things to do that my work starts to feel like work when it started off feeling like a blessing. My work *is* a blessing. God allowed me to borrow His creativity, gifts, and talents to begin my ministry. I wake up some mornings and see the blessing that is my husband. My marriage is a blessing because God extended my husband to me. The same goes for my friends, children, and parents. God is so generous toward us that something can even start off a curse and end up a blessing. A blessing is only a blessing as long as we see it from God.

The moment we begin to see the blessing as our norm, responsibility, or burden, the value begins to decrease because we no longer honor it as coming from God. If you know for a fact that your job is a blessing from God, but your boss tap-dances on your last nerve, I want to challenge you to not let that boss hijack your blessing mentality. Now, girl, don't get it twisted. I'm not telling you to be a pushover and just take whatever happens to you. I'm suggesting that when confronting whatever is standing in the way of you seeing your blessing properly, remember it all began as a blessing.

If your marriage is from God and your husband starts stressing you out, it doesn't mean that your feelings aren't justified, but I would challenge you to ask yourself if the version of you who saw your husband as a blessing is showing up in your marriage every day. How can the version of you who sees your husband as a blessing communicate what you're feeling while staying mindful that he is from God?

The same is true for every good and perfect gift that God has brought into your life. Whether it's a job opportunity, a child, a school, or a parent, we must strive to live in the consciousness that the blessing came from God. That means the solution to the dilemma can only be found when we honor that God is in it.

That's why when my husband and I counsel individuals, we're

not just looking at their history or chemistry, we're looking for the God factor—when both parties possess the irrefutable knowing that their partner is a gift from God. If a couple has the God factor, then we feel our role and responsibility is to get them to God. If we're able to handle whatever is in our relationship with that honor in mind, we will navigate our issues with honor and sensitivity because we never want to defame what God gave us. By the way, just because a marriage doesn't start with God doesn't mean that God can't become the center of it, but it does require that each person come to a place where God is the center of their character and identity.

With this in mind, the petty version of me can no longer assume that when Adam called Eve "the woman You gave me" he was throwing her under the bus. Perhaps Adam decided to make sure that even amid confusion he never forgot that the blessing came from God. This mindset is one we'll have to employ as we continue to grow and move forward. We cannot fall victim to the narrative that walking with God is akin to a stress-free vacation that will only prosper us, but rather the narrative that we've found a path worthy of sacrifice, which offers restoration and reconciliation for anything we lose along the way.

This is called perspective, but you can't have this level of perspective if you're living your life like a speed racer on autopilot. In order to maintain the mentality of your blessing, you have to insist that there's room in your life for you to be hypersensitive to the rhythm of rest, introspection, and intentional joy available to you in any given season. But it's not unusual for us to get so caught up in living our lives like we're some kind of machine, and then become frustrated when we reach our breaking point. That's when we want to just quit everything.

I believe that soul care, not to be confused with self-care, begins with taking inventory of the areas of our life where we feel a burden but once felt a blessing.

Working It Out ━━━━━━━━━━━━━━━━━━━━━━━━

Yeah . . . the journal, go ahead and grab it. Think through these questions and make notes to record your responses.

- What area of your life feels like a burden but started off as a blessing?
- What was happening in your life at the time this blessing arrived that made you feel fortunate to have it?
- When was the first time you began to feel like your blessing was a burden?
- When was the last time that blessing felt like a blessing?

Look at what you wrote. Sometimes we need to back away from our blessing so we can see it properly. There may be some areas where you could have been a better steward over your blessing, or maybe as the blessing unfolded, you experienced some surprises that detracted from the honor you had for the blessing. Is there something you need to accept, reject, or change that is clouding your vision of that blessing? Make sure as you're making this assessment, that you're not looking from the perspective of a burden but with the consciousness of it being a blessing.

━━━

When we try to fix our problems from a place of frustration, we can sometimes create more problems (example: SJR being kicked out of pretend heaven for being petty). When we choose to tackle our issues from the place of honor, our strategy reflects the honor we have for the opportunity in the first place. A job can be a blessing in one season and a catalyst for a new career in the next. Just because you're leaving doesn't mean you tell the boss how raggedy they were on the way out the door. I kid! I know you would never do that. Right? (You become the good in goodbye when your character remains intact while your presence moves to its next act.)

That sounds all good, but none of this can happen when you're stressed. When you're stressed, you don't have time to be the bigger person. When you're stressed, it's much easier to be petty than it is to stay silent. That's why the best gift you can give your soul, besides returning to the blessed consciousness, is to make sure you're making time for yourself.

It may sound ridiculous, but sometimes you need a reminder that there should be space for you in your own world. Just because you're in your world doesn't mean that you've made room for you. There are moments when our existence is relegated to living on the outside edges while we create space and a place for everyone else. While we focus on the comfort of others, we often ignore the responsibility we have to ourselves. The career must be pursued. The waist must be snatched. The home must be clean. The dinner must be cooked. The friends must be in place. The skin must be clear. The pressure is on creating a picture-perfect existence, with us as the photographer. The only problem is you become so busy creating the picture that you never step in the frame. You can't just make space for every*one* else and every*thing* else and ignore the fact that you take up space too.

There's a moment in the Bible that speaks to this very thing. In Luke 10:38, Jesus visited two sisters, Martha and Mary. Martha wanted to make sure the house was spick-and-span for Jesus. Can you imagine the pressure? While she moved busily about the house, serving and preparing things, she looked up and saw her sister Mary sitting at Jesus' feet. Martha is my petty homegirl for this because instead of giving Mary that frustrated "girl, if you don't get up right now" look, she snitched on Mary to Jesus.

She expected Jesus to reflect the men of the time and put Mary in her place as a woman. But Jesus said something surprising in response to her complaint. "And Jesus answered and said to her, 'Martha, Martha, you are worried and troubled about many things. But one thing is needed, and Mary has chosen that good part, which will not be taken away from her'" (Luke 10:41–42).

What's interesting about Jesus' statement is that He wasn't going to spend the rest of His time there with Martha and Mary. Soon enough He'd be heading to the next town. So when He said that Mary had chosen that good part, "which will not be taken away from her," Jesus was not talking about His person. He was talking about what happens when we are in God's presence.

What happens when you have a moment of prayer, meditation, intentional breathing, worship, or church? You don't stay in that location forever, but the feeling remains with you wherever you go. As often as you can, you must find time in your day to alleviate your worries and troubles and receive a steadiness that cannot be taken away from you.

YOU MATTER

Your soul matters. Your mental health matters. Your body matters. Your peace matters. Your feelings matter. You can't expect other people to see you as a priority if you don't see yourself as one. So often we make self-care about taking time to focus on ourselves, but we can engage in soul care every day by forcing the world to make room for the truth of who we are. That means when your feelings are hurt, you don't try to act tough, but let the people know you're not a punching bag. When you're too tired to go, you don't force yourself to show because you don't have a spare battery you can just swap out. When you need help, you let the words come out your mouth, and you don't wait until you have no other option. You do it before you run out of options.

Why do we ask for help as a last-minute resort? Yes, I'm preaching to myself too! I go to the grocery store, and I become the Hulk, getting the groceries out of the car by myself. I waddle into the house with the bags pressing into my skin as I try to support the unbalanced weight between my arms. Everyone starts yelling, "Why didn't you ask for help?" I would have asked for help if I didn't have it under control, but I had it, so there was no need for help.

That's exactly how we spend most of our day. We spend to the limit and only get relief when the pressure becomes too much. What if we found a way to incorporate a care regimen that doesn't require us being at our breaking point before we ask for help? I truly believe there is a difference between self-care and soul care, but I also believe the definition is different for each person.

For some people, running is soul care. It's how they clear their mind from the stress of the day. They say things like they feel free and weightless when they run. I think that is so beautiful, remarkable really. I consider running self-care. It's something I do to take care of myself, but it does not make me feel rested. I feel strong, focused, and intentional when I finish running, but I do not feel rested and relaxed. Soul care for me is meditation, reading a book, or sleeping.

I think it's important that we know what self-care is for us versus soul care. Self-care may be something that makes you feel good afterward but doesn't actually give you peace in the moment. Both are important to being balanced, and, unfortunately, neither of them seems to be easy to experience consistently.

Here's a challenge for you. Start a self-care / soul care match with someone close to you. The goal is to do one thing a day that is self-care / soul care. Instead of ending your day with the things you need to get done tomorrow, or thinking of what you accomplished, make a list of what you did for you.

I have found that when I'm not doing a good job of taking care of myself, I get very, very irritated when people start asking me to do things. And by things, I mean them asking me to fulfill an expectation that I set in the first place. Like when my children ask me for dinner, or my team asks me to respond to an email. I mean, seriously, why would these people continue to ask me to feed them and lead them when I haven't fed or led myself?

When our normal responsibilities start feeling like demands from tyrants, the good has become hard, the blessing a burden, and our breaking point is inevitable. That's when we start looking for shortcuts instead of exerting our mental capacity to problem solve. When we start looking for the easiest way to get things done, we stop innovating and begin depending on what we already know. This continues until we have about fifteen extra pounds we didn't ask for, three hundred unread emails, six children to feed, one husband to romance, a host of friends to support, and . . . wait! This is supposed to be about you, not me.

We need to get to the point where we aren't waiting to hit our breaking point before we ask for the help. I want to help us get to a place where we're able to take breaks even when we don't need them so we're not living life like in sprints—rapid bursts and then breaks—but rather with a steady, calculated endurance that allows us to preserve ourselves in the process.

You're likely asking why.

When good becomes hard, it's meant to force us to stop functioning the way we were so we can create new rhythms and paradigms. Innovation is the product of frustration. When you become frustrated enough with the way something is, you'll find a way to create a better process. This level of innovation doesn't occur until we acknowledge something isn't working, back away to identify where the malfunction is, and then reengage with a plan to stop the frustration from occurring again.

Do you know why God tells us early on in Genesis that the war of seeds will end in victory? Because God knew how to zoom out of the picture, acknowledge what this issue was, and then reengage. The entire Bible is ultimately the playing out of God's Word in the garden. Everything we read after Genesis 3:15 is how God continues to partner with humanity until the time is right to introduce seed that darkness cannot defeat.

If darkness is beginning to cloud your vision, then innovation is ready to be released in your world. Stress is a sign that it's time to reassess how you're structured. It's tempting to take a vacation and then dive back into a preexisting rhythm, but whenever possible consider if there is a better way to function that you don't currently see. What if the preexisting rhythm that caused the stress could be tweaked so you're not repeating a cycle?

Moses is one of my favorite Bible characters. Exodus depicts the story of how Moses rose as a leader to the Hebrews. At the time of his birth, there was a declaration that every son born to Hebrew women must be killed. Moses' mother was a Hebrew woman who defied this order and instead placed him in a basket and floated it down the river. His sister stood by watching until he was found by an Egyptian princess.

Moses was raised in the Egyptian kingdom, but he was a Hebrew child. His existence became complicated, so he disengaged from it altogether. He could not stay disengaged though. God needed him to return to the place of his frustration but armed with a perspective that would uncomplicate his experience. There are moments when we leave a situation because it's too challenging or complicated. When we leave the place to which we're called, we can never stay gone until our work in that place is done.

If you're reading this and you've allowed your frustration to force you to run, it's time to stop running. You can't run just because things get hard or because you start to feel like you're in over your head. You can step away, take a breath, and recalibrate, but your days of cowering down and shrinking in front of hard are over. I pray that you would come to a place of permission. Permission to acknowledge how you feel, but to not be governed by your feelings alone.

Had Moses stayed away from the place where he experienced frustration, he never would have discovered what God placed inside him. He would have ultimately been living unfulfilled because he wasn't living out God's dream for his life. I don't want you to miss out on getting to know you. You may be thinking that you're better off on the sidelines, not making any waves—but also not realizing that God sees you as a force.

Don't let the hard things trick you. You're stronger than you believe. Yet neither do I suppress my emotions and pretend I'm okay when I'm really not strong. You are a real, vulnerable, authentic, confident, revolutionary world changer who is strong because of who she is, not because of who she pretends to be. The quicker you learn how to harness your power and balance who you are, the sooner you can get to the business of exploring the depths of the strength God has placed in you. You were made to overcome hard things. When good goes hard, you go harder!

EIGHT

GOD GOALS

And Peter answered Him and said, "Lord, if it is You, command me to come to You on the water."

—MATTHEW 14:28

I grew up in church. In fact, I've wondered if I might actually have been born there—you know, like maybe back by the baptismal? Not really, but when your dad is the pastor, your family is in the building every time someone turns on the lights—with that someone being one of you.

Though I was there a lot, I was never one of those girls who studied the Bible. Instead, I depended on the church experience to learn the basic scriptures. Which is probably why I ended up thinking things were in the Bible that were not actually there. Things like "Don't be so heavenly minded that you are no earthly good" and "An idle mind is the devil's playground." These were such a part of my childhood that if mind = blown were a person, it would be me. (Maybe they should be added to an Ebonics version of the Bible.)

Actually, one of those church sayings has always made me feel a little confused. "If you want to hear God laugh, make plans." I totally get where it comes from, as I can think of the countless times when I've made plans and then what I had in mind didn't even come close to happening. But it made me wonder, what's the point in setting goals and making plans if it's unlikely that they will turn out? Do I do nothing? Not if "an idle mind is the devil's playground."

Can you see how I ended up confused? It has taken some time, but I now understand that though they are not Scripture, both of these statements are valid and important to know.

An idle mind doesn't have to be the devil's playground, but it is something like a playground. Bill Gates is often quoted as saying, "I always choose a lazy person to do a hard job because a lazy person will find an easy way to do it."[1] A mind wired for laziness is looking to get things done as quickly as possible. Before you start thinking to yourself, "Not my mind!" you should know that science is beginning to prove that primitive existence developed a method of survival rooted in the belief that the less you did the more likely you were to survive.

This way of living preserved life, but it also made humans more prone to laziness. Productivity and innovation are a result of our minds seeking the most efficient way to get things done so we can do nothing. If my life's motto could be summed up in one sentence, it would be the one you just read. I don't like feeling like my time is being wasted because of a process or system that isn't efficient. When the inclination toward laziness and necessity for productivity collide, innovation is birthed. Innovation is the result of producing a more efficient way to get something done.

Technically the idle mind is a playground, but you get to choose the owner of that playground and what you allow to be produced from that idle mind. In the process of discovering more efficient and effective ways to get things done, there will no doubt be times when your plan fails altogether, but a new, more refined plan emerges.

I was listening to a TED Talk that referenced X (formerly known as Google X), an American semisecret research and development facility and organization founded by Google in January 2010 that rewards its employees for failing.[2]

In a BBC article, technology editor David Grossman wrote that at this special lab "inventors and engineers are encouraged to collaborate on audacious ideas."[3] This may not sound particularly unique, but what makes the environment for creativity different is that it is devoid of the conventional reactions to failure.

Astro Teller is the team leader at X. In the BBC article he said, "You must reward people for failing. If not, they won't take risks and make breakthroughs. If you don't reward failure, people will hang on to a doomed idea for fear of the consequences."[4]

STEP OUTSIDE THE BOAT

This unique approach to innovation provides some balance as to why making God laugh with your plans isn't something you have to avoid at all costs. While your mind is busy producing, creating, and planning, don't allow the idea that your plan may not pan out the exact way you have in mind keep you from producing at all.

If you've come to a place where you've accepted your identity as an extension of God on Earth, it may take some time for you to figure out exactly how you're supposed to show up and where you will be most effective. That means there may be moments when even your best efforts end in failure. Failure is not a curse word, and even when we fail in the pursuit of what God has for us, we have a promise that it will all work out for our good.

Have you heard the story about Peter, one of Jesus' disciples, attempting to walk on water? Jesus' disciples were in a boat in the middle of a storm. Right in the middle of them losing it, Jesus appeared and told them to be calm even though the storm was raging (Matthew 14:28). I'll paraphrase, but Peter's response was basically, "God, if that's really You, command me to come to You." As in, Jesus, don't stop the storm, but allow me to walk through the storm the way that You are doing.

There's a whole sermon in that, but stay focused. Jesus commanded Peter to come to Him, and for a split second Peter began to walk on the water. Unfortunately he took his eyes off Jesus, and the moment he did, he began to sink. Jesus rescued him from drowning and placed him back on the boat.

There's much conversation about how Peter didn't have enough faith, but I can tell you he had more faith than I would have had in the moment. He may not have completed the task the way he had in mind, but he did accomplish something he would have never accomplished had he not challenged himself in the first place.

Why is this important and what does it have to do with your journey? I want you to begin making goals for yourself without fear of failure or of the unknown. I want you to come to a place where you are content with starting to head in the right direction and that you don't get caught up in whether you'll reach the desired destination.

If the disciples had been anything like my siblings, when Peter was alone, they would have been clowning him for not being able to keep walking toward Jesus. Nothing would have been off-limits in the commentary, from the way Peter trembled when he saw he was sinking to how he even thought he could do it in the first place. Imagine having an audience while you step out on faith when you're still battling uncertainty; the possibilities of failure are high.

You may hear a chorus of voices from people in your circle with their own set of commentary as it relates to your goal, but do you know what the other disciples will never be able to say to Peter? They will never be able to say that they know what it's like to step on water. He may not have been able to accomplish his goal, but the mere fact that he attempted the goal set him apart from anyone who could have negative feedback about what he attempted. In addition, Peter learned something about Jesus that none of the other disciples were brave enough to learn.

Don't allow the fear of what other people think keep you from spreading your wings. What you're called to do may be different from the circle around you. No one but you and God may understand that for some time, but what matters is that you and God have that understanding. That's you! If our goal is to become more and more like the image of our Creator, we're going to have to step out of what we know and begin seeking out what God knows.

I feel like there's someone reading this book and God is saying that He has something He wants you to know about Him that He hasn't shared with anyone around you. You won't discover this revelation by staying in the boat. You will only come to this revelation by stepping out and away from those who think they know you so that you can figure out what God truly knows.

Sometimes we think that we need to step away from people forever while we pursue what God is commanding us to do, but the truth is that there will be instances when you only need to step away long enough to get a revelation. Peter gets back in the boat. Peter keeps walking with the disciples. Peter keeps connecting with the world around him, but he is not the same Peter he was before he stepped out of the boat. Peter and Jesus have an insider understanding that only the two of them know. Maybe you just need to step away from your circle long enough to get some inside information about who God is and what God can do with you.

Working It Out ━━━━━━━━━━━━━━━━

It's journal time in the sanctuary! Let's set some goals.

Think about your life and create goals that fit within three specific categories—

- short-term,
- long-term, and
- generational goals.

Let's start dreaming. (This sounds good to me already!) By the way, don't worry if you don't have a goal for every category. And though I love those little internal goals that only require internal accountability, don't stop there. Get big, bad, and bold in your dreaming. List whatever comes to your mind. With that, here are some things to consider when thinking through and writing down your goals.

1. Your generational and long-term goals don't have anything in common with your now. That's why it's a goal. Don't limit your goal to your now. When a goal comes to mind and you start thinking about how it's impossible for whatever reason—just don't go there, don't do that. That's a major cop-out! And it makes me give you *major* side-eye.

2. Take inventory of your now. What do you want to do with your tomorrow? Where would you like to see yourself in five years? What would your goal be if you weren't afraid it would sound too ambitious or crazy? What would your goal be if money and support wasn't a factor? Go 'head with your bad self! Take the limits off your potential.

Keep that page open—we're going to return to it. First, there are a few things I want to share with you about the goal categories.

1. Your short-term goals determine whether you'll accomplish your long-term goals. If you have a long-term goal, but not a short-term goal, then your long-term goal is just a dream. There should be something you're doing today that will help get you one step closer to that goal tomorrow.

2. I try to connect my long-term goal with my generational goal. I consider the generational goal as the new way of existing that I want to establish for people influenced by my journey. That could be family, friends, coworkers, and/ or mentees whom I desire to be exposed to a new model. If your long-term goal only gives you gratification, then you're robbing the world of the positivity it so desperately needs. Generational goals are my way of saying that I recognize my life is bigger than me, and what I do each day doesn't come down to affecting just me—it affects the generation that is alive to see my journey.

3. An example of a generational goal may be, "I want to create generational wealth in my family." You can write this goal and have thirty-five cents in your bank account. That's fiiiinnne! What I really want to know is what short-term goal are you

implementing that will make your generational goal inevitable? The same type of connection is also beneficial in helping with our short-term goals. If we have a short-term goal of losing ten pounds before a party, we should consider asking ourselves if there's room for expansion within that goal. One potential area of expansion is wanting to normalize a mindset of generational health and wellness. With the short-term goal married to the generational goal, your motivation to continue progressing becomes about the new normal you're attempting to establish.

RENEW YOUR MIND

Nothing underscores my belief in God like the study of our bodies and how they function. I'm by no means a scientist, but when I'm on a quest for information, I most often begin by uncovering undeniable evidence that God is the Master Artist and is strategic in everything He creates. As I began studying the brain and how it responds to goal setting, I was even further convinced that setting goals is one of the tools God gives us to renew our mind.

The University of Texas conducted a landmark study on patients with multiple sclerosis. Multiple sclerosis (MS) is a disease that affects the brain. Some of the symptoms of MS include impaired speech, loss of muscle coordination, numbness, and severe fatigue. The study revealed that patients who set goals for wellness experienced less severe symptoms than other participants. Setting goals quite literally healed their brains.[5]

If you're struggling to get the willpower to activate progress toward your dream, then this should be good news to you. By beginning to set short-term goals, even if you have to set them day by day and not weeks or months at a time, you are giving your brain an opportunity to be rewired. When your goal is so far beyond where you are, it can be challenging to feel motivated to even start working toward it, but when you break down that goal into bite-size pieces, it gets much easier.

Wanting to save $50,000 may sound impossible, but if you start off by saying you're going to skip Starbucks today and move the money to your savings account, you're adding a drop to the bucket. And every drop counts. You'd be surprised how you begin to respond when simply being in process is more important to you than the finished outcome. Science is proving that the moment a goal is set (and I mean actually set, not just talked about), a portion of the brain begins to accept it as finished. This is why our brains chemically respond to the failure to meet a goal with a similar reaction to the distress we experience over the loss of a valued possession.

That just helped someone recognize why a breakup is so hard. Sometimes it's not so much the person you're missing, but rather the loss of the goal you thought the relationship would reach. When we fail to achieve any desired outcome, whether it's for our health, relationship, finances, or business, two neurotransmitters that exist in our brain are immediately affected: dopamine and serotonin.

Dopamine is directly connected to the feelings of satisfaction and accomplishment we experience when we've set a goal. Serotonin is the neurotransmitter that plays a key role in helping us maintain our mood, appetite/digestion, sleep, memory, and so much more. Now you can see how the inability to meet a goal can send our moods spiraling in so many different directions. It also underscores what the University of Texas study has already revealed—our goals can change our mind.

No wonder Paul wrote in Romans 12:1–2,

> I beseech you therefore, brethren, by the mercies of God, that you present your bodies a living sacrifice, holy, acceptable to God, which is your reasonable service. And do not be conformed to this world, but be transformed by the renewing of your mind, that you may prove what is that good and acceptable and perfect will of God.

Paul wrote this letter to the church of Romans. The church was positioned to be one of the most influential of the time and produced the first generation of Christians who would set the standard for every generation to come. Paul admonished the church to make presenting their bodies to God as the goal. Then he wrote that it would be less than ideal if the goal was presented with the same ideology of the culture. At that time Rome was polytheistic, wealthy, and powerful, which was the standard, but for them to follow the teachings of Jesus, they would have had to submit to the process of transforming their minds.

- Short-term goal: Present your bodies as a sacrifice to God.
- Long-term goal: Be transformed by the renewing of your mind.
- Generational goal: Prove what is that good and acceptable and perfect will of God.

When studying the word *prove* in Romans 12, I learned that it was translated from the Greek word that literally means "evidence." Your life is supposed to be evidence (for the generations) of the good and acceptable and perfect will of God.

Examine your personal goals again. Are there any categories where you can fill in the blank? Can you take your short-term goals and begin to make them bite-size and manageable? The hardest part is getting started from there, but all you really must do is sit back and allow the inevitable outcome of sticking to your goals to show up in your life.

I truly believe Eve made this her "secret sauce." Let me remind you of the curse in Genesis 3:15:

> And I will put enmity
> Between you and the woman,
> And between your seed and her Seed;
> He shall bruise your head,
> And you shall bruise His heel.

God gives Eve a goal in this scripture. Let's dig in to that next.

RECEIVE THE SEED

We've already discussed how the battle between the woman and the serpent would come down to seed. The goal is to produce seed, but there's a little fine print that God doesn't mention. The fine print is that God doesn't tell Eve which seed will be the Seed who will bruise the head of the enemy. The only thing He makes clear is that it will begin with her but will end with a he.

This scripture is God's way of letting the serpent know that there will be redemption through a man. He doesn't say when or how; He just continues to lay out the consequences of eating from that fruit. After that moment, Eve has her marching orders. Had she stayed stuck in resentment or shame, she may not have found the courage to start setting goals that would bring the victory God spoke of in Genesis 3:15. Eve found a way to allow the goal God placed in front of her to become more powerful than the decisions behind her.

Can you begin to see how I came to a place where I found beauty in Eve? Honestly, if I can't see the beauty in Eve, then I can't recognize the beauty in me. Why? Because we all have to make a similar decision to the one that she made. We will have to abandon the decisions of the past and reach for the hope of tomorrow. This is not a decision we make without intentional goals and plans. The hope of tomorrow is buried in the seeds of today, but seeds don't sprout without work, and work cannot be deemed effective unless there is a goal attached to it.

Eve's responsibility was to acquire seed. Biologically, we know that men are deemed the carrier of seed; however, the text reveals to us that the prophecy requires the woman take ownership of the seed.

What is seed? *Seed* is the Word that God gives us regarding our destiny. *Seed* is the Word of God. This isn't just about Scripture, though Scripture carries the Word of God as well. This is about how God communicates with His creation that is different from how His creation communicates among themselves.

Receiving a word from God is different from receiving a word from man, although God can use man to deliver His word. When you receive a word from God, it bypasses your mind and hits you in your soul. It's a word that brings a part of you to life that you didn't know existed. If you've ever been through a hard time and had friends try to lend support or encouraging words, some of them sound routine, but every now and then a word moves beyond your feelings and emotions and lands right in your soul.

That word is the word God placed enough weight on that it broke through your walls. God uses His word to accomplish everything He does on Earth, so when God makes a declaration, that declaration will come to life when it's regarded as valuable to the person who receives it. God didn't just give Eve a possibility of what would happen. God gave Eve a guaranteed outcome of what would take place.

The seed of the woman referenced in Genesis 3:15 is Jesus. Later in the Bible, when speaking about Jesus, John wrote:

In the beginning was the Word, and the Word was with God, and the Word was God. He was in the beginning with God. All things were made through Him, and without Him nothing was made that was made. In Him was life, and the life was the light of men. And the light shines in the darkness, and the darkness did not comprehend it. (John 1:1–5)

This text brings to light the inextricable correlation of seed and word. Jesus is called a seed in Genesis but a word in John. Later on, in John 1:14, what began as a word became flesh: "And the Word became flesh and dwelt among us, and we beheld His glory, the glory as of the only begotten of the Father, full of grace and truth."

There's a cycle here that must be acknowledged so it can be applied to our own lives. God gives seed, the seed becomes a word, the word becomes flesh and dwells with us. That means there is an expectation for the seed to grow until it becomes the word. You'll know that you've graduated from seed to word when you begin building your life on the principle of that word. Jesus is quoted in Matthew 4:4 saying, "It is written, 'Man shall not live by bread alone, but by every word that proceeds from the mouth of God.'"

The implication here is that when we begin to live our life, we're living it based on the word that proceeds out of God's mouth. Sometimes we're looking for someone else's words to deliver our breakthrough, but we fail to realize that we can get a breakthrough whether the person speaks the words we need to hear or not. Your breakthrough is not contingent on what comes out of their mouth. Your breakthrough is contingent on the word on which you build your life.

I don't know about you, but I have tried to build my life on the words of other people, and each time I failed. But there came a moment when I realized the only way I could build my life is if I allowed only God's words to become my truth. I wasn't sure what God was saying about me specifically, so I started working the words He'd given to other people over time. Words that assured me I am "fearfully and wonderfully made" (Psalm 139:14), reminding me I was made with care and respect. God didn't just throw me together in any old way.

God thought about everything I would need to come into this world and make change and endowed me with everything I needed. If God took His time to make me with care and respect, and I turn over what God made to someone who doesn't see the care and respect God placed in creating me, then it's my responsibility to remove myself from the situation. I only allow relationships and opportunities in my life that are a reflection of the word I'm using to build my life.

I don't think there's any pain like the pain that results from a parent not valuing the life God entrusted them to care for. Parental wounds are the most painful because having them makes you question whether or not you should be cared for and respected. I grew up in a two-parent household where there was no abuse of any kind. We laughed, we loved, and my parents did the best they could. But, still, I didn't escape having parental wounds. Over the years I've heard stories from people whose parents abandoned, rejected, betrayed, and abused them.

It made me realize that whether your household was like mine or was much more toxic and painful, we all experience parental wounds. I think it's because we're all supposed to come to a place where we're able to turn the wounds over to God. God blessed you before your parents failed you. God never wanted you to experience the wounds you have from your parents, but those hopes shifted in the garden. The hopes shifted, but they weren't destroyed. God can't change what you experienced, but He can bring you to a place of healing and freedom that makes it possible for you to recover as if it never happened. That goes for any area of your life in need of restoration.

All that begins by taking hold of those words and allowing them to become seeds, word, and then flesh. It may just be a seed right now, but I believe that as you're reading this book, God is watering that seed. You're going to close this book, and someone is going to come along and say something to you that adds some sunshine to that seed. You're going to pick up your phone, and there's going to be a message that adds oxygen to that seed.

You keep working that seed until it becomes word, and when that word becomes flesh, you'll understand why God told Isaiah, "No weapon formed against you shall prosper" (54:17). God never promises that the weapon won't form. He doesn't promise that you'll never see the weapon. All He promises is that the weapon won't have its intended use.

Some of you have had weapons formed before you even knew who you were. The weapons began when you were in your mother's womb and followed you throughout your childhood. The weapon had a plan to blur your eyes from seeing God's truth about who you are and His vision of your identity, but the weapon didn't know you were going to keep searching, reading, believing, and hoping that there was more to you than what you've been through.

No more than the weapon could prosper against Eve in the garden can this weapon prosper against you. So what did Eve do when the weapon had been formed and the seed had not yet been watered? She didn't focus on the weapon. She started working her seed. You don't have to attack the weapon that's forming against you. All you need to do is work your seed. Your seed will outwork your weapon.

Eve had tunnel vision on the seed. The seed was going to be what restored her confidence. The seed was going to be what gave her back her power and authority. The seed was going to drown out the voices of shame, regret, and disappointment. The word that God gave Eve specifically was directly connected to her producing biologically. It may or may not be necessary to say that not every seed is about biological production. Some seeds are about books, ministry, nonprofits, business, education, relationship, mental, emotional, and spiritual health. We have the seed God gives to all humanity, and then we have our specific seed.

Whether you're at a stage where you're working the seeds God has given us all, like coming to a place where we believe we're fearfully and wonderfully made, or God has given you a word regarding your destiny, I'd like to utilize the life of Eve to demonstrate how she worked the goal of bringing what God said to manifestation.

NINE

SET IT IN MOTION

*And Adam knew his wife again, and she bore a son and
named him Seth, "For God has appointed another seed
for me instead of Abel, whom Cain killed." And as for
Seth, to him also a son was born; and he named him
Enosh. Then men began to call on the name of the LORD.*

—GENESIS 4:25–26

I never thought I would come to a point in life where I would even
consider that I need to be more like Eve—but then I studied how
she bounced back from her major setback, and that's when I realized
#shewasgoals.

Eve managed to stay connected to the mission even after she
and Adam were kicked out of the garden and began living outside
of God's original plan for their lives. There is nothing like a woman
intent on making God's plan for her life a reality. By the way, that's
totally you too. Eve didn't allow the consequences of her actions to
keep her from recognizing that there was still a promise hanging
over her head.

That felt like a word for somebody.

Whether your trauma has been self-inflicted or imposed by another person, there is still a promise hanging over your head. When you begin positioning your life for the promise, you start setting the promise in motion. This is exactly what Eve did when she found herself adjusting to her new normal. She made the bold decision to move her promise with her into her consequence.

That felt like *another* word for somebody!

Just because your circumstance changes doesn't mean that your promise can't move with you. We need to be so committed to the promise God has given us that even when the promise shifts, we don't abandon it.

THE PROMISE FOLLOWS US

Have you come to the place of faith where you believe without a shadow of a doubt that the promise cannot be eradicated by the circumstance, but that the promise is even more anointed because of how far it has to go? Nothing in your life may look like what God said, but isn't that always the case? What we see versus what God sees are two completely different things. When you've made a commitment to make God's vision your vision, you may have to close your eyes and work.

I really feel like this is what Eve does in Genesis 4. She closes her eyes and starts working toward what God promised her. She comes to this bridge that each of us will have to cross at several points of our journey. Can you be committed to what God said even when your attempt doesn't look like what God said? Before you just say "Yes!" without taking a moment to think, I want to challenge you to dig a little deeper.

We think we can stay committed, but when the attempt has your blood, sweat, and tears mixed up in it, it can be hard to just volunteer to try again. Failing at something you don't really care about is one thing, but failing at something that you were betting would bring you closer to God's promise is a completely different thing.

Eve set in motion exactly what God said. She started producing. Genesis 4:1 tells us that Adam knew his wife and she bore a son, Cain, and then she bore again and had Abel. At that point she had come into alignment with what God said her focus should be, and she started producing based on that place of alignment. The only problem is—and if you don't know how the story ends, this is going to be a major spoiler—Cain killed Abel.

Can you imagine what that moment must have been like for her? She was finally doing everything the right way, but what she produced didn't look like what God said. It seems like we should be able to go from God spoke it, I obeyed it, and it came to pass, but anyone who has ever attempted to do anything that requires faith knows that more often than not there are moments when our effort doesn't look like what God said.

This is where I learned how important it is to commit to a process and not just the outcome. This is part of the reason I believe in the expansion of goals. When we meet a short-term goal, the long-term goal continues to keep us motivated. But if things happened overnight, there would be no need for discipline.

Discipline is about coming to a place where we're no longer entitled to outcomes but rather expect them because they are the organic product of the effort we expend each day. It's the most underrated character trait. By the way, it's easy to require a character trait from another person when it's one that we've mastered ourselves, but when we aren't sure that we possess it, we'd rather not mention it at all. I feel like this is how we handle discipline.

No one is entirely sure how well they can discipline themselves until they actually try to do it. For instance, I may be disciplined when it comes to one thing but struggling in another area. I'm learning that discipline is not a state, but rather a process of correction. When we lack discipline, what we're actually lacking is the ability to correct the patterns we know should change. We have an outcome in mind, but the outcome is not attainable without discipline. And discipline cannot come without correction.

When Cain killed Abel, he revealed to us that the outcome Eve had in mind would not be attainable unless she was able to withstand the pain and discomfort of her seed being corrected so her outcome could be effective. Discipline is about fine-tuning the outcome. As a parent, when I discipline my child, it's because I want to see a different outcome from the one I'm experiencing. When God disciplined Cain, He wanted to change his outcome. I love a good tirade about haters every now and then, but not everyone is hating on us. Sometimes people are trying to correct us, but we're too fragile to receive the correction, so we push it away. When we push it away, we fail to realize that we're also pushing away the outcome that will help to further manifest our journey.

This is an instance where we could aspire to be more like Eve. Eve had enough discipline not to quit. She proved in this moment of unmet expectation that her trust in God's Word couldn't be dissuaded just because the first outcome didn't reflect what God said. Eve had made a commitment to set the word in motion. If the outcome didn't look like what God said, then she'd be bold enough to try again until something in her life looked like what God said.

I'm one of those people who try to dissect every outcome to

determine if something could have done something better. I feel like if I have ownership in the demise, then I can have wisdom in the rebuilding. Conversely, if there's nothing I could have done better, I take peace in knowing that I did all I knew to do given the information I had.

It's with this approach that I looked at the difference between Eve's first attempts at producing seed versus what we know ultimately happened with her third son, Seth. As I studied the breakdown between Cain and Abel, I identified that the area where things fell apart had to do with Cain not being able to handle correction from God. That's when things got heavy for me.

HANDLING CORRECTION

Adam and Eve demonstrated how to handle correction when you know you've done wrong—they handled the consequences of their actions. But how do you handle correction when your intentions are pure? No one likes the person who can't own up to their mistakes, and if we're honest, there are some days when we are that person.

I love hearing people talk about their love languages. Thanks to the incredible book *The 5 Love Languages* by Gary Chapman, we've been able to take the time to dissect how we give and receive love. I think it would be a unique experiment to take the time to contemplate our correction language.

Have you ever considered the way that you give and receive correction? We have no problem letting people know we aren't perfect, but imperfection is not an excuse to make no effort to move toward better. If we can live with the knowledge that humanity is imperfect, then we should also consider taking the time to evaluate the best way we want to receive and give correction.

There is a difference between criticism and correction. Criticism has a tinge of meanness connected to it and often comes from a person who may not have your best interests at heart. Correction is when someone loves you so much that they want to make you aware of a tendency you have that could be limiting your growth. I learned about my own struggle with correction in the relationship that guarantees to school you about yourself 24/7: marriage.

When my husband and I were first married, there was no room for him to challenge me to think or act differently in any area. I couldn't quite figure it out at first, but eventually I came to the place where I realized I was unable to receive correction from him because I could not separate his feelings for me from his correction of my actions. (There are layers to this, so just stick with me.)

I think my history with toxic relationships made me feel like there's something I could do to change my husband's affection toward me. My fear of him seeing me differently made it difficult for me not to become defensive when he brought up an area where I could have handled things differently. When I say that it was difficult, I mean that my eyes would roll, I would suck my teeth, and I would give off an attitude so thick it could be considered a force shield against nuclear weapons.

One day when we weren't in the throes of a disagreement, my husband finally asked me, "Why is it so hard for you to receive correction?" Being defensive is a natural response for me, but because he caught me off guard, I had no choice but to go within to answer the question. I learned something that may help you or someone you know who is like me.

Being a teen mom is the closest you can get to wearing a scarlet letter. From the looks in the grocery store to the stares at church, walking around as a young woman with a baby attached to her hip felt like walking around with a sign that read, "I was wrong." This created a subconscious desire to stray from anything that had the appearance of wrong. I lived with the idea that because I had this "wrong," I could not afford to be wrong again.

I forced myself to pursue an unrealistic standard of perfection as the thought of more failure became unbearable for me. I needed to work on that. I started with dissecting what it was I felt when I was called out for being wrong. When I boiled it down to shame, I knew the little girl in me was having the response, not the woman who knew her worth wasn't based on a perfect performance.

I believe that within every woman is (or has been) a little girl looking for acceptance, love, and evaluation. That littler girl shows up at the most inopportune times and has a tantrum or fit when she feels she's being misunderstood. Once I realized the little girl in me was having the visceral reaction to being wrong, the woman in me had to evaluate the correction I was receiving. I'll give you a silly but honest example because, at this point, we're friends.

I'm writing this book at the height of the COVID-19 pandemic. The only way I can get enough quiet to tap into the writing zone is to hide from my children. I hide by escaping to a balcony in our house that has been unfurnished for about three years. Little do they know I've slowly been sneaking furniture to the balcony, essentially making it my apartment. I go to the balcony and get lost in the content of the book. Eventually, they find me and begin knocking on the door, asking me about chicken nuggets, batteries, and whatever other random things they can think of.

My husband told me the other day that I need to make sure I lock the door when I come back inside. Before the woman in me could even respond, the little girl started thinking of the eight thousand times he left the door to the balcony unlocked. Fortunately, I managed to pull the little girl back before she could tell my husband about his own failures. Instead, I looked him in the eye, said he was right, then assured him that I'd try to do better next time.

Somebody needs to send me a box of chocolates or something for the level of maturity I displayed because everything in me wanted to reverse the correction. I'm trying to come to a place where I don't need someone else to be wrong so I can be right. I'm learning that it's okay to be wrong even when you have the best intentions.

Working It Out

Eve did the best she could with what she had left, but I think the greatest test she faced wasn't with the serpent but in how she responded in this moment. I think it's time we get the journal and begin examining how we receive and give correction. Maybe you're not like me and you don't struggle with receiving correction, but you have been accused of being a little rough in giving the correction. Your intentions are good, but could your delivery be better?

1. First things first. Jot down the last time you were wrong. How did you learn you were wrong? How did it make you feel? Angry? Ashamed? Hurt? Misunderstood? What would you have done differently armed with the knowledge you now have? Did you apologize to the person affected by your decision?

This is the part where so many of us stumble. We figure out what we did wrong. We even decide what to do next time, but we never go back to fix it. God didn't get upset with Cain for offering a less respectable sacrifice than Abel. God gave him an opportunity to go back and fix it. "So the LORD said to Cain, 'Why are you angry? And why has your countenance fallen? If you do well, will you not be accepted? And if you do not do well, sin lies at the door. And its desire is for you, but you should rule over it'" (Genesis 4:6–7).

There's nothing wrong with being wrong. Having the ability to acknowledge and fix your wrong builds trust. It's much easier for us to think of ourselves as the victim than it is for us to consider that we've been a villain. Think about all the people who have done something wrong to you. Now consider how much peace you would have if they sincerely realized the impact of their decisions, apologized, and attempted to fix it. There are some people you could never imagine coming back to do that. I'm sorry they hurt you. I wish they realized the impact their decisions had on your heart and soul. The greatest gift you can give your future is not to let that spirit of ignoring the pain you've caused live on through you.

If you're thinking of someone right now who you know you did wrong but never fully owned up to it, perhaps you should consider acknowledging to them the role you played in their brokenness. The admission of wrong does not mean your intentions were malicious. If the relationship is still amicable, but this has become an elephant in the room, then move the elephant out of the way and make room for healing to come. Don't let your pride stand in the way. Some relationships are too far gone, and the damage has been severe. Reaching out may cause more pain, trauma, or discomfort. We don't want to do that. In those instances, I think there are two options worth considering—you can either write the person a letter or just be content with praying to God for their healing and restoration.

If the opportunity ever presents itself for you to express the wisdom you've learned since inflicting the pain, then you'll know it was in God's plan for you to repair what has been broken. The most important thing you must remember, regardless, is that you're not asking the other person to make you feel better about what you did. You're acknowledging to the person that you understand what you did. This is not a step you should take when you want the person to make you feel less guilty. This is a decision you make when you are so full of love and compassion for yourself and others that you would never want anything that the lesser version of who you are did keep someone in bondage. I'm sure you've heard plenty of people say, "Forgiveness is not for the other person; it's for you." We use this often when we are victimized, but when we have created the victims, I think this holds even more power.

And when you ask for forgiveness, don't do it so you can regain favor or position in someone's life. Do it so you can replace the poison you injected with love. Think how wonderful it would be if we all came to a place where we were able to withstand the discomfort of being corrected without it changing our view of ourselves or others.

2. If you've still got that journal handy, take a minute and also consider how you would have preferred to hear that you were wrong. This is an incredible conversation starter that everyone should consider having in any relationship. Asking these types of questions moves the relationship from being about something more than "How can I love you?" and toward the deeper question, "How can I grow with you?" Growth doesn't occur without correction.

I asked all the Woman Evolve team members to take a personality test before joining the team. It was instrumental in helping me understand how to communicate with them. It revealed to me the best way to help them grow and how to make sure they are celebrated for their contributions to the team. Whether you're leading a business team, raising children, connecting with friends, or learning to love your significant other, the most important gift you can give them is the gentle care of their heart.

The more comfortable we can become with correction on Earth, the less punished we will feel when God says no. Hebrews 12:6 says, "For whom the LORD loves He chastens, / And scourges every son whom He receives." I'm not going to lie—I wish there was a better word than *scourges* for this text, but I couldn't let this point rest until I underscored that even your relationship with God will experience moments of correction. As a matter of fact, the conviction you feel when you know you're doing something you're not supposed to do, and then pay the consequences later, is God correcting you.

That correction doesn't mean that God doesn't care about you anymore or that you've lost your place in God's heart. It's actually quite the opposite. It means that God loves you so much that He doesn't want to see you out here wrong. He wants to see you live a life guided by His spirit dwelling inside you. In Hebrews, the Greek word *scourge* means "to whip." See why I wanted a better word? Don't nobody grown or little want a whipping! Yet because we are guaranteed to do something wrong, we must accept that there will be moments when learning to do better come because we didn't do well the first time.

Almost a full chapter goes by before we see Eve's promise begin to take the shape of what God said. Eve had good intentions for her seed, but her seed could not withstand correction. What was the difference between Cain and Abel and then Seth? The difference came down to Seth's son calling on the name of God. This reveals to us that God wasn't just looking for someone who would offer Him the right sacrifice. God was hoping to establish a relationship with humanity that wasn't about what they did or gave but rather how they wanted God to be a part of how they lived.

KEEP PRODUCING

Not many things are clear in the original curse declared that day in the garden. There was no timeline on when things would play out. It's unclear how Eve would produce seed or how her seed would transform to His seed. The only thing that *is* clear to us after God speaks to the serpent in Genesis 3:15 is that the serpent would experience defeat. Obviously, Adam and Eve partaking of the fruit also lets us know that for the serpent to be defeated, humanity is not crafty, strong, or wise enough to do it on their own. They need a power greater than what they possess.

That power will ultimately come from humanity's ability to partner with God. That's why what happens with Seth's son Enosh is so important to the manifestation of the promise. Eve set out to accomplish the goal of producing seed, but her experience revealed that the seed would be successful only if the seed was able to partner with God every step of the way. "And as for Seth, to him also a son was born; and he named him Enosh. Then men began to call on the name of the LORD" (Genesis 4:26). In the original Hebrew, the word for *call* actually means "encounter." Adam and Eve encountered God in the garden, but each generation would need to encounter God so the seed could become word and the word then would become flesh.

I wonder if you could be like Eve when it comes to your seed. I wonder if you could make a decision that just because the seeds you produced in the past didn't become what you had in mind, you won't allow that to keep you from producing seed. Eve must have decided within herself that she wouldn't stop producing until her seed looked like what God said.

As you're reading, I have an important question for you to think through and answer for yourself. *Do you have what it takes to throw another seed in the direction of your destiny?* Because here's the deal. Until Eve's seed had an encounter with God, she had to keep producing. Abel's encounter was cut short. Cain's encounter was revoked. But Seth bridged the gap between what failed and what would succeed. Enosh's encounter was the confirmation that what Eve set in motion would continue on Earth.

Let's talk this out. You're not just setting in motion an encounter for yourself. You're setting in motion generational encounters for your family. What happened in the garden was not just about Adam and Eve. What happened in the garden was about humanity. The serpent wanted to thwart humanity's ability to have an encounter with God, but the serpent didn't know that Eve was going to roll up her sleeves and do whatever was necessary to rebuild what had been broken. That's why there's been a war over you being able to manifest what God placed down on the inside of you. It's not just about you; it's about the legacy of healing, wellness, and destiny that will be available to the generations connected to you.

For a second, I almost felt badly for Eve. I mean, after all, she didn't get the chance to see the enemy get the final blow we know he received in the New Testament, but when I was studying, God gave me a revelation. Eve didn't have to see the final outcome because she set in motion the inevitable.

Remember when we talked about your goals and how when we commit to our short-term processes then our long-term goals are inevitable? That's exactly what I'm saying here. The next time you start doubting that you won't be alive to experience that generational goal, I want you to talk back to doubt. Sometimes you have to tell doubt, "I may not be the one who sees the final outcome, but I will for sure go down as the person who set it in motion." Don't make this journey about where you finish. Make this journey about where you start.

Where you are right now didn't just start with you. It began with what God set in motion with someone who came before you. Somewhere a teacher, parent, grandparent, neighbor, or friend placed a seed inside you, and that seed got buried. For some time, it seemed the seed may have even been dead, but while your life was going up and down, the seed was still there. The seed was waiting for the moment it could take root and produce fruit so it could start a revolution inside of you.

As a black woman in America, I connect deeply with this truth. Not a day goes by that I wake up and am not reminded of those who came before me who could only dream of the luxuries we have today. It would be foolish of me to think that what I enjoy now began with me. I realize that my present circumstance started long before I got here. My reality is the product of intentional work to make sure that the color of my skin didn't determine where I sat on a bus, whether I could vote, or which water fountain I could drink from.

Those who led the civil rights movement knew their cause was bigger than them and that if they were able to accomplish what was inside of them, it would change everything that came after them.

The same is true for you as you embark on this journey. This is bigger than you. This is about what you're going to set in motion on Earth. Where do you want to see breakthroughs in your way of living, thinking, believing, giving, and receiving? I'm praying that God would highlight the area where He has ordained you to win.

When God placed air in your lungs, it was the equivalent of cashing in all your chips at a high-stakes table (terrible analogy but stick with me). God doesn't just think you can set His plan in motion; God knows that when you come into alignment with what He's doing, your community, family, church, career, and entire sphere of influence will become better too.

The first thing I want you to hear in the morning is "Set it in motion!"

When discouragement and fear start whispering in your ear, I want your faith to yell back, "Yeah, but I'm still going to set it in motion!"

Just like my ancestors set in motion my present, Eve set in motion a lineage of humanity that calls on the name of God. Theologians believe there were sixty-three generations between Adam and Jesus. That's sixty-three generations of humanity calling out to God and God responding to humanity.

Throughout the Old Testament we see how God designated men as prophets to represent mankind. Those prophets carried His word and called upon God's name. Then one day about two thousand years ago, when man called on the name of God, He didn't just engage with a prophet but wrapped Himself in flesh and came down to Earth.

This is it! This is the moment we've been waiting for since Genesis 3:15. This is the seed that would bring restoration to humanity. We cannot see Eve in Genesis 3:15 without seeing the silent character hidden between the text. God never makes mention of her, yet the seed cannot be produced without her. This woman is Mary, the virgin mother of Jesus. Mary represents the culmination of what Eve set in motion.

As much as Genesis 3:15 is a foreshadowing of Jesus, it is also a foreshadowing of Mary. There is an inextricable connection between Eve and Mary that hit me in my core. Imagine that whenever you've had a moment when you knew better but didn't do better, that was also a hidden opportunity for restoration. Mary is Eve's ultimate restoration. When Mary gave birth to Jesus, she set in motion a series of events that allowed humanity a direct connection with God. But she also closed the chapter on what took place in the garden.

I can identify with Mary as much as I can identify with Eve. I've been given the precious opportunity to be a facilitator of what God wants to do on Earth. This book is evidence of that.

I believe that in every woman is an Eve and a Mary. There's a version of us who knows better but doesn't always do better. Then there's a version of us who has enough faith to say yes to whatever God asks her to do.

It's hard to say who has the most power from day to day, but no doubt a version of both women lives inside us all. I hope that last sentence offered you some modicum of peace. There will be some days when you straight up don't feel like being the bigger person and rising above. You're going to know that you should, but you are not going to be excited about it. Those are the days when Eve may be having her way in your life. Just remember that when you feel those days, even Eve recovered and decided to get back in the game.

Then there will be other days. Days when you find the beauty in saying yes. Moments when you are so overwhelmed by what God has trusted you with that all you can do is sit back and take it all in. Those days, when your life is surrounded by the majesty of God, those are the days when you look most like Mary.

TEN

DON'T DO IT ALONE

Blessed is she who believed, for there will be a fulfill-
ment of those things which were told her from the Lord.

—LUKE 1:45

Mary and Eve shared a lot of similarities. Both women's plans were disrupted. Both were given the responsibility of producing seed. Both had partners who helped them facilitate what God needed to do through them. Both women's existences represented a threat to the enemy.

There was also one stark contrast between them: Eve was aware of why she had been chosen, but Mary was not quite sure.

We're getting close to the end of this book, but I can't allow you to close it without telling you that there are moments coming that will make you wonder why God chose you to behold His majesty. It only takes a few experiences with disappointment to come to a place where it's easier to expect disappointment and tragedy than to expect God to blow your mind. Regardless of the variation of trauma you've experienced, we're all left in a similar state of distrust. The sting of the pain lives with us and becomes more real to us than the possibility that better could ever occur.

That doesn't keep us from wanting relief or hoping things get better, but when better actually occurs, sometimes it's hard to come to a place where you feel worthy and deserving of what is right in front of you. It has been said that it's better to give than to receive. This is especially true for the person who doesn't know how to receive at all.

If this is you, consider opening your heart and mind to this concept. I want to bring you to a place of great expectation. I want to give you permission to expect beauty out of life again.

For some of you, the mere idea feels like getting your hopes up after you've already been let down so many times, but if you're still on this earth, there is something good for you to behold. If you can come to the place where you're comfortable with expecting good things again, one of my prayers for this book would be answered. I'm praying that you would begin to believe that greater is coming *and* that you're worthy of receiving it. It's hard to believe that we're worthy of greater when our actions have caused us to believe that not only are we not worthy, but, because of our history, we cannot trust ourselves either.

When you look back over your life and you see moments when you expected better, but better didn't come, you learned to no longer trust your own heart. When you pursued a plan for which you were passionate, but the plan didn't turn out as you'd hoped, it trained you to not trust your passion. You can trust God with all of your heart; the true question is, can you learn to trust your heart again even after you've given it to God?

I don't know about you, but I've trusted God with half of my heart to even just some of my heart, but my ultimate goal was for God to yield to what *I* desired. It wasn't until I trusted God with *all* my heart that I could trust the heart God gave back to me.

Sometimes we talk about trusting God with "all of our heart" like that represents the level of strength we're placing in giving our heart to God. But when you slow the words down and say them intentionally, you'll see that what we're really saying is that we trust God with the entirety of our heart and all that it possesses. When we turn our heart over to God after it's been damaged, wounded, and abused, it's because it needs surgery. It's not because our heart needs to be tucked away in a safe. God brings our heart to a place of healing, perspective, and restoration, then He gives us our heart back and says, "Woman, evolve! You can trust who you're becoming because you trusted Me with your becoming."

GOD WANTS TO HEAL YOU

I'm reminded of a woman in the Bible who had an issue with her body that caused her to constantly bleed. For twelve years she tried everything she could to get the flowing to stop, but nothing worked. One day she heard that Jesus would be walking through her town, so she decided she would try to get to Him.

She pressed through the crowd and managed to get close enough that she was able to touch the hem of his garment. When she did, her flow of blood stopped immediately. She received the healing she needed, but her encounter with Jesus didn't end there. Jesus called out to the crowd, "Who touched me?" The woman, so used to hiding, did not respond immediately, but Jesus would not let the moment pass. The woman recognized she couldn't stay hidden and revealed her identity. The woman had already been healed, but Jesus spoke these words to her: "Daughter, be of good cheer; your faith has made you well. Go in peace" (Luke 8:48).

The woman had been healed of her issue of blood before Jesus spoke these words, but there was another healing her soul needed, one that she didn't even know she needed. The customs of those times deemed the woman "unclean" because of her issue. Being ostracized and perhaps made to feel unworthy caused the woman to lose her cheer. We don't know who she was before her issue, but some of us can remember who we were before our own. We were happier, more optimistic, ambitious, and full of faith. Our issue changed that.

Sometimes the only way to survive after we've had an identity-shifting experience is to change the way we show up in the world. The woman with the issue of blood had to become someone in order to live with her issues. She had to become someone who didn't mind being on her own. She had to become someone who understood the world saw her as unclean. She had to be willing to shrink into a shell of who she could be because of the ever-present reality of her condition. Her encounter with Jesus healed the issue, but when Jesus gave her permission to have cheer, another healing occurred.

The woman's heart was wounded when she came to Jesus. After the encounter, He gave her heart a new expectation, a renewed sense of hope. God wants to do the same for you. The woman's journey wasn't complete until she had a moment when she was standing in awe of God's power not only to heal her but to see her as worthy of having joy and peace. God wants the same for you.

I want you to come to a place where you trust that you deserve to stand in wonder at how God wants to change your life. This will require a level of surrender to goodness that you might never have experienced.

We've learned to cower down and surrender to fear. We've learned to shrink and surrender to anxiety. Far too often we've allowed our-selves to surrender to an energy that didn't build us up or make us better. That surrender created a rhythm that makes us more comfortable shrinking than trusting. When joy knocks on your door, you'll have to surrender. When hope comes, you'll have to surrender. Give yourself permission to embrace that the possibilities are working in your favor whether you see how they're working or not.

This is exactly why Mary's life is so important to this revolution you're embarking on. Mary had to surrender her plan so she could lay hold of God's more excellent plan. That sounds so easy to do, but when you're not sure why you've been chosen, or if you can even imagine the journey ahead, it's easier to reject the goodness.

You know I wouldn't be me unless I gave you my personal story of coming to a place where I surrendered to the beautiful life God was bestowing upon me. Remember how we talked about me going on tour? Well, I did all the preparation with my partner. We produced the content, hired the crew, and sold the tickets—and the response blew me away. Everyone was so excited, and it appeared the tour would be a success, but inside I was terrified.

I felt like I had nothing worthy or valuable to say. It was easier for me to plan and execute the vision than for me to stand and trust in the vision. It was the Sunday before we launched our first seven cities. We'd only be gone for ten days, but I was beginning to believe I'd made a mistake. I started listing all the reasons why this moment shouldn't be happening for me.

The Saturday before our departure, I was packing my bags while also reading through my "résumé of wrong" when the words I heard as a teenager stung my heart afresh: "I always knew to expect something like this out of you." A family friend uttered that to me when the news of my teen pregnancy could no longer be kept a secret.

I attribute these words to the reason it was difficult for me to trust God's love was still available to me. It's also the reason it took quite a bit of time before I learned to trust myself again. I felt the sting of being Eve, and it's the only way I saw myself for many years.

The problem with seeing yourself only as Eve is that it's challenging to come to a place where you believe you're capable of making good decisions. No matter how many subsequent decisions you make, you run the risk of seeing your life through the lens of the decision that upended your life.

The failure to trust ourselves shows up in how we engage with the world. When you don't trust yourself, you impose a punishment that serves as a constant reminder that you didn't do better. What's even worse is when the suspicion you're not worthy of trusting yourself is confirmed by your environment.

I didn't intend to get pregnant. I didn't intend to cause anyone pain. I definitely knew better, but I didn't do better. Nevertheless, I wanted someone to let me know in the middle of all that was going on that I still had goodness and virtue inside me. That was the moment I stopped trusting myself. That was the moment I no longer believed the expectation of goodness was something that could happen to me.

Sure, I continued to work like I believed I could one day escape the image people had of me. The image that I held of myself. When I remembered those words, I instantly became that little girl again, but this time I was packing and heading out for a tour. I felt small. Tiny. Inconsequential. Powerless. I felt like Eve, but everything in my life was suggesting I was Mary.

Well, you know, I'm nobody's quitter, so I didn't cancel the tour just because I was in my feelings, but the sense of inadequacy spread through my soul like an infection, and I wasn't sure I had anything worthy to say. The Sunday we left for the tour I couldn't help but open myself to worship. There have been times I didn't dare open my pain, too afraid I couldn't find a way to squeeze it back in the box I keep it in. That Sunday I had no choice; I was desperate to stop the aching and be affirmed by God.

Whenever I'm in a moment like this, I break out of the habit of routinely singing the lyrics to the song and take a moment to truly let the meaning of the words rest on my tenderness. Worship songs that remind me of God's faithfulness and restoration have always hit me in my core. That day the lyrics soaked into my soul like water in a desert. Tears filled my eyes while my heart fought to find the truth. I kept thinking of thousands of women who were coming because of what God could do for them through me, and the tears flowed. My insecurity said I had nothing to give them. Then something incredible happened. The same words that had ripped me open performed surgery and healed me back up. As I imagined the faces that were expecting God to flow through me, I heard God's voice speak so clearly, "I always knew to expect something like this from you."

Those same words that once had torn me to shreds now brought me to a place of wonder. When I was pregnant, depressed, divorced, and distressed, God was there waiting for me to figure out who I was so I could walk into this moment when He trusted me to carry His glory. I only saw myself as Eve, but God saw me as Mary.

TRUST WHO YOU ARE IN GOD

Have you ever considered how the situations you've faced and experiences you've survived shaped your view of self? I mean more than feeling broken or damaged, have you ever contemplated whether you truly trust you are still worthy and deserving of facilitating God's glory on the earth?

Looking back, I realize the most damaging thing that happened to me had nothing to do with what happened *to* me and everything to do with what happened *inside* of me. I didn't realize it until much later, but somewhere along the way I stopped trusting myself. When you don't trust yourself, you live in a perpetual state of second-guessing, but more damaging than the questions is how you perceive your heart, character, and integrity. It is possible to believe in others, believe in God, but not believe in yourself.

Call it the culmination of my failures or the combination of too many mistakes, but the outcome of my decisions convinced me that I could not be trusted to make my way in the world with my damaged heart.

I didn't realize that when I was giving my heart away, it was because I didn't feel like I could trust myself with myself. Even giving my heart to God was a result of me feeling like I couldn't trust myself anymore. This is the beautiful place of surrender we all must come to, but we are not meant to stay in a place of distrusting ourselves.

When God begins to work in us, and then through us, we can begin to trust who we are in Him. I may not be able to trust who I am in my fear or who I am in my insecurity, but I can trust who I am in God. Trusting my heart in the past had led me to put my heart on clearance and lower my standards. When I trusted who I am in God, I didn't mind passing up temporary company when I was awaiting constructive partnership. When I trusted who I am in God, I could stand up to anything that stood in my way without puffed-up ego or pride, but with the knowledge that God was working in me.

When the lowest part of you finishes dictating your thoughts and actions, you can turn your heart over to God, but you must be prepared for the moment He gives it back to you.

YOU ARE BLESSED

Some time ago my dad wrote the book *Can You Stand to Be Blessed?* I was too young to read it when it released, but as I'm typing this chapter, I can hear the title ringing so clearly in my mind.

I want to confront the part of you that will set goals, execute visions, trust God's provision, but then go to bed at night wondering if you truly deserve God's blessing. The short answer is no. You don't deserve it—none of us does. Yet God doesn't relate to us based on what we deserve, or Adam and Eve would have been dead on arrival the moment they ate from the fruit. God deals with us based on how He sees us.

When the angel of the Lord came to Mary, she had to be willing to lay aside what she thought she knew about herself so that she could discover what God knew. Mary's initial response to the visitation from the angel gives us insight into how she perceived the honor of being chosen to carry glory.

> And having come in, the angel said to her, "Rejoice, highly favored one, the Lord is with you; blessed are you among women!" But when she saw him, she was troubled at his saying, and considered what manner of greeting this was. Then the angel said to her, "Do not be afraid, Mary, for you have found favor with God. And behold, you will conceive in your womb and bring forth a Son, and shall call His name JESUS." (Luke 1:28–31)

The angel's greeting suggested that Mary should begin rejoicing, but the text lets us know that instead of rejoicing she was troubled. Because we know how this story ends, we can understand why she would be troubled by the idea of being a virgin mother, but take another look at the text. The angel didn't tell Mary that she was going to give birth to the Messiah. All the angel said was that Mary was highly favored and blessed among women.

History tells us that Mary was an ordinary Jewish girl, but this text lets us know that she was only ordinary by man's standards. By God's standards, Mary was highly favored and blessed.

To embrace the reality that you are blessed among women, you have to break out of the mentality of thinking you're ordinary. That doesn't mean other women aren't blessed. It means that you have been blessed among women who have also been blessed in their own ways.

CELEBRATION NOT COMPETITION

For years, the narrative has been that women don't get along. I don't know that I fully believe that it's true, but I do know that women often compare themselves to other women. I think the comparison occurs among sisters, colleagues, and friends. It isn't always mean-spirited or vindictive, but it's subtly present. Comparison is so dangerous because we're measuring ourselves by someone else's results when we didn't have their start.

Because we often find ourselves in comparison, it's much easier for us to feel inadequate compared to other women's blessings than it is for us to feel blessed among those women. I never fully understood how powerful Luke 1 is when it comes to two blessed women learning to honor and respect each other until I studied how Mary and Elizabeth engaged after they both received unexpected blessings.

Elizabeth was Mary's older cousin. In Luke 1:36–37, we learn about the miracle pregnancy she was granted. When Mary had her visitation with the angel, she wasn't aware that her cousin had also had a visitation and was pregnant until the angel of the Lord told her, "Now indeed, Elizabeth your relative has also conceived a son in her old age; and this is now the sixth month for her who was called barren. For with God nothing will be impossible."

You're going to want to pull up the Bible app on your phone, or grab your Bible if you have one near, because I want to point out some things that happened when Mary had the encounter that revealed God had chosen to favor her among women. You should read the entire chapter of Luke 1 if you really want to keep up, but for the sake of time you can cut right to Luke 1:39.

The angel had departed, and Mary had surrendered to the favor on her life. *Bloop!* I'm mad I just wrote in one sentence what took me about eight paragraphs to explain, but that's the part right there that I'm trying to prepare you for: the surrender to favor. When Mary finally surrendered to the favor, she didn't just sit in the place where the angel met her; she went to find Elizabeth. Why? Because favored women need other favored women.

The reason the narrative that women don't get along can continue to permeate the culture is because our natural inclination to comparison keeps us from authentically celebrating one another. Mary couldn't just go see another woman in her city to share this news. She knew that she needed to be in the room with another favored woman. You have got to get in community with other women who see you worthy of celebration, not competition. If you don't have a room like that, then *you* have to become the celebration in the room.

Some of our friendships are only healthy because we're sick. When you're sick, you find someone else who understands your disease, and you bond over that pain. But then you also get together, sit in the corner of the room, and point out the flaw of every woman who walks in because that's how you handle yourself.

If you haven't come to a place where you can celebrate another woman, you can get in a room with other favored women and still feel awkward and out of place because you aren't sure you belong. This isn't just about changing your friend circle; this is a challenge to change how your friendships circle. You may be the champion your community needs. You can become the cheerleader in the corner of every woman pursuing her goal and not just of the women you prefer.

Working It Out

I want you to grab that journal you've been writing in and make a list.

1. List the names of the first three women who come to mind. It doesn't matter how random they are or what your relationship is like. I'm not asking you to write down the names of women you respect or admire but, literally, just the first three names that come to mind.

2. Now write down one thing you feel they are gifted to do really well. It can be the way they speak, dress, love, support, build, or save.

3. Once you've done that, I want you to consider whether they realize the amazing gifts they have.

Whether the answer is "I'm sure they know," or you think they may have no clue, I want you to understand the power God has given you to affirm another woman in what God has given her. What if the encouragement that another woman needs is locked inside your mind because you think she already knows it or that it won't mean much coming from you?

Maybe you aren't able to galvanize your crew toward change, or maybe you don't even have a crew at all. Consider getting plugged in to a network of like-minded women who carry the same passion to seek the best versions of themselves. These women may be at your gym or at your church—you can even get plugged in to the Woman Evolve community. Whatever you do, make sure you're in an environment where greater expectations are the norm and becoming better is the organic rhythm that leads your community through life.

BE THE CONFIRMATION

I know without a shadow of a doubt that community makes a difference. No one understands what it's like to be a woman more than a woman. After hosting event after event with powerful women from all over the country, I'm more convinced than ever that when women get together, powerful things take place. Don't believe me? Let's go back to Luke 1.

Mary was on a mission to get around another woman who could understand her favor. The text tells us that she headed to Judah with haste. My girl Mary wasn't wasting any time trying to get plugged in with someone who understood what she was up against. Chiiillle, Mary didn't even have to spill the tea to catch Elizabeth up on what happened because the moment she opened her mouth, Elizabeth already knew that something was going on.

> And it happened, when Elizabeth heard the greeting of Mary, that the babe leaped in her womb; and Elizabeth was filled with the Holy Spirit. Then she spoke out with a loud voice and said, "Blessed are you among women, and blessed is the fruit of your womb! But why is this granted to me, that the mother of my Lord should come to me? For indeed, as soon as the voice of your greeting sounded in my ears, the babe leaped in my womb for joy. Blessed is she who believed, for there will be a fulfillment of those things which were told her from the Lord." (Luke 1:41–45)

You know what's so amazing about Elizabeth's response to Mary? She confirmed that what the angel said *would* happen *had* happened. If you look back at the conversation between the angel and Mary, the angel didn't say that Mary was pregnant in that moment. The angel didn't even say when she would get pregnant. The angel simply said that it was going to happen.

It's not until Mary had the encounter with Elizabeth that we recognize Mary had stepped into what God promised. That's not where the exchange ended though. Elizabeth confirmed Mary's pregnancy, but Mary also made Elizabeth's baby leap and then filled Elizabeth with the Holy Spirit. Some theologians believe Elizabeth's baby was no longer living, and that the baby leaped because the power of what Mary was carrying invaded what was trying to die in Elizabeth.

I'm going to be straightforward with you. As I'm writing this book, I have one goal and one goal only: to either make your baby leap or confirm what God is doing in your life. Imagine if we as women took on the responsibility of not just becoming someone worthy of being honored and admired but becoming the kind of woman who makes every woman feel honored and valuable.

That may require you to not allow your pride or ego to walk in the room before you do. Even so, I guarantee you will never lose when celebrating another woman's success. If you had to, you could go at this alone, but it would be a terrible injustice if you robbed another woman of the support and encouragement that could push her to the next dimension.

Whether it's a stranger on the street or a lifelong relationship, create an opportunity to celebrate the strength of the women God allows you to cross paths with. The road ahead for Mary and Elizabeth would be challenging. The Scripture doesn't tell us much more about how they interacted or when they saw each other again. We do know that Elizabeth gave birth to John the Baptist, who would later baptize Jesus, yet the only documented interaction between Mary and Elizabeth is detailed in Luke 1—the gift each of them needed.

You'll have some encounters that are not meant to be lifelong friendships. I told my husband that I think the notion of BFFs is as romanticized to young girls as the notion of fairy-tale endings and Prince Charming. We want so badly to hang on to friendships for a lifetime. That may not be everyone's story, but we can make sure the time we've been given leaves a beautiful impression on someone's life forever.

ELEVEN

WILD WOMAN

"I make known the end from the beginning,
from ancient times, what is still to come.
I say, 'My purpose will stand,
and I will do all that I please.'"

—ISAIAH 46:10 NIV

Ninety-three women are recorded to have spoken in the Bible. Of those ninety-three women, forty-nine of them were named. Most of the women mentioned are heralded for their faith, courage, and bravery. They are considered matriarchs of our faith and the type of women we should aspire to become.

The Bible seeks to tell the story of God's love and restoration for His creation. It's the reader's responsibility to connect with the people mentioned throughout the text. Sometimes I wonder if my disconnect with the Bible reflected my not being able to see myself. So often I felt unsure of myself and my faith in comparison to the more popular women we've come to celebrate. All that changed when I had a chance to study Eve. She is the mother of all living and the mother of every woman. If we reject her for her mistakes, then we will most certainly reject ourselves when we make mistakes.

As we seek to take up our space in our worlds, we must never forget the value of representation. To see glimpses of yourself in Scripture and to watch God's faithfulness to that person is to understand how God can connect with you now. It is equally important that you recognize you are someone's representation.

I was channel surfing and came across a documentary about Danny Trejo, a Latino American actor who overcame adversity and became a Hollywood film star. I'm sure you've probably seen his face. In the documentary he spoke about being a young boy and seeing Mexican American actor Pedro Gonzalez Gonzalez on TV. At the time, he had seen people who looked like him only play characters who were in jail or on the streets. He didn't realize there was another path until he saw another Hispanic man on television.

As a black woman, I understand how lack of representation can limit your ability to gauge your potential. While watching the Trejo documentary, it dawned on me that lack of representation does affect everyone. I'm telling you this because I think it's important you realize that you are someone else's mirror.

The footprints that led you to this moment are so similar to where someone is standing right now—they may never find their way if you don't become their guide. When we come to the realization of how interconnected we are, we recognize that our confinement does not affect just us; it also affects people we can't even see. I could have never imagined that you would be holding this book when I was in my darkest days. I didn't think our worlds would collide; I was too busy assessing the damage from my collisions. Yet here we are. I didn't know, but God knew.

MARY CAME FIRST

I always thought that what happened in the garden with Eve paved the way for Mary. Then I read Isaiah 46:10, which helped me see that God already knew what would happen in the garden—so Mary came first. Before the woman was deceived by the serpent, her redemption had already taken place. Before the woman ever ate from the fruit, her restoration had already been sealed.

Likewise, before I was the little girl who felt out of place in a very big world, in God's mind you were already holding this book, and I'd already found the place He put on reserve for me.

It's time for us to say goodbye, but before our journey together comes to a close, I want you to know that there's a place on the earth that has been reserved with your life in mind. Your destination hasn't been canceled nor has it been denied. You may have found your place once but somehow lost your way. That place is still yours, and because you're still here, there's an opportunity for you to get back to your place and experience the life God had in mind when He created you.

You already know that life may not be smooth sailing. There may be moments when it's downright tough, but being effective at the reason you were created is much more fulfilling than having a life that doesn't rock any boats.

You're ready. You're more ready than you've ever been. Girl, the mere fact that you've made it to the end of this book is a sign that you don't mind putting in the work.

I've shared a lot with you here. Some things may have struck you to your core while others may be for you to revisit at another time. Begin the work now by taking what has stuck out the most to you and seeing how you can begin to implement it into your life.

Give yourself grace as you learn to walk in this new way, but be intentional about where you're headed and the environment where you place your seed. As you begin working this journey, God will continue to highlight areas where a little stretching will take you a long way. History is not done being made. There are so many firsts that still need to be written, and allowing your light to shine is the only way to make it happen.

ANOTHER WOMAN

When it comes to actual women in the Bible, Eve and Mary will always be the greatest of all time for me. But there is another woman I want to introduce you to before our time comes to an end. This woman is not an actual woman but rather a manifestation of a vision that John had while on the island of Patmos.

Most theologians see the vision of this woman as a representation of the church. When I read this story, I couldn't help but see it as quite literal because the woman represented this beautiful combination of Eve and Mary. The woman in this passage does not have a name. This woman is every woman. This woman is me. This woman is you. Now, I must admit that this woman is in the Bible's most unnerving book, but we're not afraid of scary things. That's who we used to be.

Grab your app, or open your Bible, and journey with me to Revelation 12 to meet the woman who now sets the tone for what's possible for you and me.

The story begins with a celestial woman appearing in the sky, pregnant and in pain. That's normal for us now, but that was not always God's plan. Pain in childbirth became the woman's consequence for what took place in the garden:

To the woman He said:

"I will greatly multiply your sorrow and your conception;

In pain you shall bring forth children;

Your desire shall be for your husband,

And he shall rule over you." (Genesis 3:16)

The woman in Revelation, with her hint of Eve, was bearing the burden of another woman's curse. So are we, but this woman also carried the breakthrough that Eve wasn't able to see.

That will be your testimony too. It doesn't matter how many generations have been affected by what you're now up against. When your chapter comes to an end, you won't just be carrying your breakthrough—you will be carrying the breakthrough that the generations before you were not able to experience. The woman wasn't only navigating the residue of Eve's curse; she had an adversary, a gold fiery dragon, waiting to devour whatever she produced.

The vision continues, but the woman's story transitions from mirroring Eve to reflecting Mary's story. In Revelation 12:5, we see that she is pregnant not with an ordinary child but with a child that is to rule over all nations. That should have been the moment when the story came to an end, but the story takes an interesting turn because the child she gives birth to is swept up to heaven, but the woman remains on the earth.

I struggled with this abandonment of the woman and the preservation of the child, but I believe I have a perspective that will be helpful for you as you begin to produce against all odds.

The woman was not left alone to fend for herself. There was a designated place reserved for her where she was protected, provided for, and sustained: "Then the woman fled into the wilderness, where she has a place prepared by God, that they should feed her there one thousand two hundred and sixty days" (Revelation 12:6).

I want to share with you something that will seem politically incorrect, but I believe it's a necessary mindset that you must possess. Please note that this scripture does not indicate that where the woman was located became the place God prepared for her. For the woman to find her place, she had to run from the opposite direction of her fear.

TIME TO RUN

It's time for you to run, my friend. It's time for you to let the wind hit your face and wipe away your tears. It's time for you to unleash your faith and run away from the place of insecurity and inadequacy that threatens to devour your seed. God will most certainly meet you where you are, but God will never keep you where you are. Sometimes we have to stop asking God to change our present and instead ask him to unshackle us from the need to stay when we've been called to run our race.

I can imagine the woman in my mind, running with passion but into the unknown. Can you imagine how she had to work to stay focused on where she was headed? Can you imagine how she had to coach herself not to give up and keep pressing forward? Can you imagine what it was like to run into the wilderness while still needing to recover? I know you can because we've all had to run at some point, but this time will be different because this woman has allowed us to borrow her story.

We're not running just for the sake of running. We're running because we know there's a place God has prepared for us—who wouldn't run in that direction? The woman is not running in an environment that is perfectly safe, without potential for cuts and bruises. On the contrary, the woman is running in the wilderness where most people can barely survive. A wilderness is defined as an uncultivated, uninhabited, and inhospitable region. But she didn't let that keep her from running anyway.

Working It Out

While some of us may not be headed into an actual wilderness, we have been chosen to live in conditions not always hospitable to faith, purpose, creativity, innovation, vulnerability, and authenticity. Let's wrap up your final journal assignment by identifying our wilderness.

1. You are being called to transition into a way of being that feels uncultivated, uninhabited, and inhospitable. What is that place?

    For some, living in a space of vulnerability feels like being in a wilderness. For others, starting a business or going back to school feels like the wilderness. You may choose to stop advocating for everyone else and finally start to look at your own soul, and that feels wild. Whatever your wilderness is, I want you to label it.

    Your wilderness is going to introduce you to a new version of yourself. It's okay to feel different and new. You need that. You need the challenge of being out of your comfort zone so you can break up the predictability of your life. Isn't it funny how we get bored with predictability but are also uncomfortable with change?

2. Instead of bracing ourselves and waiting for the next wave of change, we are going to vow to become change.

   In your journal I want you to write down why your wilderness is important to your development. You should know that there is scientific research that proves that when faced with learning a new skill, your brain actually produces new cells.

   There used to be a belief that you're born with however many brain cells you have and that's it; however, we now know that the human brain is more malleable than once believed. That means you don't die with the same amount of brain cells you're born with. As your brain is confronted with new things, it produces more cells.

This is no different from what science taught us regarding patients with multiple sclerosis. As you head into your wilderness, you're not going to be the same woman. You'll be wiser, smarter, stronger, and more compassionate, empathetic, and confident because you dared to do something new. The wilderness may be uncultivated, uninhabited, and inhospitable to someone else, but when it's the place God has prepared for you, then it doesn't matter who else wasn't able to stay there. All that matters is that God kept the place on reserve for you. Don't allow the failures of other people to dictate your success. You may be doing something wild and crazy in someone else's perspective, but that's only because they don't understand that God has destined you to be a wild woman.

BECOME WHO YOU WERE MEANT TO BE

For the woman in the Revelation vision, the place God had for her was a physical location. I believe this may be the testimony for many of you branching into industries and fields where the type of woman you are is not always welcomed. I want to offer another definition I believe transcends any professional, economic, or relational destination that could be a part of your destiny. This is an inner place that offers you the most alignment with God.

By the time you're reading this book, it will be almost five years since I've released a book. The last time I wrote a book was in 2016. I was in an awkward phase of my life. I had a newborn daughter and was living in a new city, adjusting to my role within our church community, and discovering my voice as a speaker. That book was called *Don't Settle for Safe: Embracing the Uncomfortable to Become Unstoppable*. The book was named appropriately because everything in my life at that time was uncomfortable, and I knew I could only discover my new identity if I was willing to let go of the life I once lived and embrace my new normal.

In that book I shared what I was learning, but I was still very unsure of where my place was. Between then and now so much has changed, but the greatest change I experienced took place inside of me. This book holds the steps to how I was able to find my place. I'm sure my role and function may change over time, but the core of my character, integrity, and confidence has been established.

As you continue reading in Revelation 12, you see that the woman didn't stay in her place. She got knocked out of alignment. But when life began to shake her up, she knew that the only way to overcome was to return to the place where she felt most connected to God and more alive than she had ever felt possible.

You're going to have these moments when you have undeniable peace and joy. You'll feel confident in the decisions you make and the plans you're pursuing. You'll feel perfectly aligned with your Creator. When those moments come, I don't want you to bask in them without taking a moment to jot down your habits, routines, and thoughts.

You need to mark the spots in your habits and routines that allow you to feel most aligned with the highest version of yourself. When you finally know where your place is, it gets easier and easier to return there. The hardest part of the journey is learning where home is for you, but once you know where home is, it can't be taken away from you.

In Revelation 12:14, the woman is no longer in the place where she is being sustained and nourished. The dragon that she thought was gone returns to antagonize her, but she doesn't face off with the dragon; she faces off with herself. She realizes that it's not about the dragon—it's about her not being where she is supposed to be.

I grew up in church where blaming everything on the devil was easier than taking responsibility for our actions. When we finally realize that defeating our demons is about becoming everything we're meant to be, we'll stop having fights that distract us when we could be in environments that develop us. I wish I could say that better. Your growth is the only proof you need to give your enemies. When you step into your identity, some things can no longer have power over you.

Never be afraid to ask God repeatedly, "Where is my place now?" No matter how many times you've discovered it, if you begin to sense you're not thriving the way that you once were, you can ask for guidance. That's why documenting your wins is just as important as dissecting your failures.

The woman in Revelation discovered her place the first time by fleeing, but the second time when the dragon came to persecute the woman, God gave her wings so she could soar back to her place. Remember when I told you that once you've found your place, it gets easier and easier to return? The first time, the woman fled on foot. The second time, she was given wings.

We get discouraged when we were once doing well and don't think we can get back to that place. I want you to know that God will accelerate time, and what felt like a long journey will become a short flight because you live with an awareness that you didn't have before. No matter what wilderness you face, there will always be a place where God has ordained your survival.

There's a saying that's been around for quite some time: "A woman's place is barefoot and pregnant in the kitchen." This notion that a woman was most valuable in the home permeated the culture up until the 1960s. In the 1960s, the women's liberation movement began, and the goal was to expand the mentality regarding a woman's offerings to extend beyond what she could do in the home.

When God created the woman, he created a helper comparable to Adam. God did not create a footstool—he created an equal being. The women of the liberation movement were on a mission to redefine their place. This was a wilderness if ever there was one, but one they knew they must conquer for women to be able to evolve. We're sixty years from the launch of that movement, and women are still moving into uncharted territory that has never been open to women before.

The first female African American tactical jet pilot in the United States Navy is Lt. j.g. Madeline Swegle. In July 2020, she received her wings. Did you see that? What happened to the woman in Revelation is taking place today. God is still giving out wings. There are still firsts that must be accomplished, and God believes you are the woman for the job.

When God needed a woman to help liberate slaves, He used Harriet Tubman. When God wanted to expand who was allowed to vote in America, He used Susan B. Anthony. When God wanted the atrocities of the Holocaust to be documented for the world, He gave Anne Frank a diary. When Liberia needed their first woman president, God raised up Ellen Johnson Sirleaf. When the indigenous people of Guatemala needed an advocate, God gave Rigoberta Menchú a passion to protect her culture. When God needed a woman to set the redemption of history in motion, He chose Eve. When God needed a place where His glory could be shielded and protected, He interrupted Mary's plan. God was using women from the very beginning, and God will be using women until the very end.

These were all ordinary women who recognized that their existence held value and weight even if the communities they were in didn't see it. God is raising you up to be the first of your kind. Wear your identity with pride because no one else can do what you do. You are, without question, worth the work. If these women could do it, then you can do it too.

When you partner with God, you are given access to His resources. You access His power, creativity, and authority on the earth. That means if fear is standing in your way, all you have to do is unleash the God in you. When Eve eats from the fruit, enmity begins, but when Mary gives birth to Jesus, the victory begins. Living in the mentality of that victory is the greatest gift you can give yourself.

HIDDEN WINGS

Everything that held humanity back from connection with God and robbed us of our ability to manifest His original intention for our lives was put to death on the cross. Now our only job is to walk out that victory. There's one last part of the journey of the woman in Revelation that I want to share with you.

> So the serpent spewed water out of his mouth like a flood after the woman, that he might cause her to be carried away by the flood. But the earth helped the woman, and the earth opened its mouth and swallowed up the flood which the dragon had spewed out of his mouth. And the dragon was enraged with the woman, and he went to make war with the rest of her offspring, who keep the commandments of God and have the testimony of Jesus Christ. (Revelation 12:15–17)

In case you're wondering how we went from a dragon to a serpent, there's no explanation in the text. The only thing that happens between the metamorphosis of the dragon into a serpent is that the woman received wings. I've always felt like this underscores that scripture about what was done with evil intent actually worked out for good. The dragon started chasing the woman, but the dragon didn't realize that the wings on his back would be used to accelerate the woman back to her place.

The woman becomes so confident in her place that the serpent can no longer harm her. The serpent even attempted to drown the woman where she was, but God used His resources to spare her. Suddenly, in verse 17, the serpent becomes a dragon again, not to face off with the woman but rather with the woman's offspring.

Sometimes the enemy of our destiny is counting on our ignorance. It's counting on the fact that we may not know it's possible to
have victory over disease, depression, corporations, and oppression.
The systems that oppress people are only successful when the people
feel they have no other option. But every now and then there comes
a person who doesn't mind stepping out of line to get things done.

That person recognizes that for change to occur, you can't always
stay in the place where people are most comfortable seeing you. I
know this may not sound very pastoral, and for some people it may
sound downright ridiculous, but I didn't write this book to help keep
you in line. I wrote this book so you could recognize that you're a part
of a kingdom that has come to destroy the works of every power that
dares to keep people marginalized, damaged, broken, or confused.

It's important to note that you cannot be a part of a revolution
that you haven't experienced. When "Simon Peter answered and
said, 'You are the Christ, the Son of the living God'" (Matthew 16:16),
it's not because Peter thought Jesus had power. It's not because he
wondered if Jesus could heal the sick.

> Jesus answered and said to him, "Blessed are you, Simon Bar-
> Jonah, for flesh and blood has not revealed this to you, but My
> Father who is in heaven. And I also say to you that you are Peter,
> and on this rock I will build My church, and the gates of Hades
> shall not prevail against it." (Matthew 16:17–18)

Peter knew without a shadow of a doubt that when you resist
what you think you know and choose to figure out what God knows,
the impossible becomes possible.

Like Jesus called Peter, I'm calling you out of the boat. I'm calling
you to accept the greatest mission you'll ever accept. I'm calling you

to pursue your desire to become more and transform the world. Do whatever it takes to pick up the broken pieces of your life so you can go out into the world and let other women know that the bruising is not the end.

EVE'S STORY IS OUR STORY

I needed to tell Eve's story because Eve's story is my story. I need the world to know that she may be most known for what happened in the garden, but it's who she became after she was shattered that created a revolution. Who you become after this is more important than what landed you here. You can count on me cheering you on from my corner of the world.

I'm praying for every woman who has ever felt stuck, unworthy, uncertain, and unsure. I'm praying for every woman who has ever ventured into wild places and forgotten her way home. I'm praying for your heart as it heals and your mind as it changes. I'm praying for the generations that will be changed because you finally assumed your mission. I may not know your name, and I may never behold your face, but when I wake up in the morning, I carry you in my heart, and I keep you in mind as I develop my vision.

My purpose is to make sure every woman is awakened to the seed God has placed inside of her because the woman is usually the last to know that she's the soil. What you allow to take up space in your heart matters. Fear, insecurity, rejection, and abandonment may be living in you, but it cannot stay. Once you know it's in you, you've got to decide that it cannot stay. Girl, you got a world to change. You've got a you to become and a tomorrow waiting on you to get this show on the road. Pack up all your second-guessing and oxymorons and trust that God will handle them as you go.

You're a beautiful combination of sweet and sour. You're spicy and savory. You're Mary and Eve. You're completely understood and an enigma waiting to be revealed. You're limitless in your potential and the most divine creation. You cannot be defined, and God's power in you cannot be dismissed. You're a woman with more curves on the inside than could ever be reflected on your frame. You're neither boring nor random but strategic and powerful.

You're the answer to the earth's prayers and the greatest hope I have for my daughter's care. You make me proud to be in the skin I'm in. Your laughter sets my soul free. Your tears break my heart in the most necessary places. It makes me tender to your plight and proud of your flight. I wrote this book because you are the woman I once was and the woman I have yet to become.

This is not the end for us—this is just our beginning. This is the aftermath that takes place once babies have leaped and spirits have been filled. You will go your way and I will go mine, but our paths can never be separated because they've been so beautifully intertwined.

Before the pages run out, and this farewell comes to an end, there is one more seed I cannot withhold. You were not born to stay there or here. You were created to thrive everywhere God calls your feet to tread. It's okay for you to run. Run without fear, my friend.

My final prayer is that you would see that you were born to bring light to the darkness, a revolution of faith to the next genera-tions, and a smile in the wild. And when the fear tries to creep in and the anxiety fights to find a way in, when the hope of this book feels more distant than near, remember these two words, but read them as a command. *Woman, Evolve!*

Now, go change your world!

ACKNOWLEDGMENTS

I've been marinating on the content of this book since the moment I got the revelation about Eve at a women's conference in 2017. You never could have told me that the revelation would grow beyond a musing to a movement. There are thousands of women who've signed up to embark on this journey of evolving with me.

In my heart they're called the delegation, but in my spirit they are my sisters and greatest inspiration. Some have been with me since I was blogging in 2011; others are just connecting with my voice for the first time in this book.

No matter where you are on the journey, I want you to know that you are the reason God allowed me to survive. I am forever grateful that you made room for me in your life and on your journey. Your support of Woman Evolve is a constant reminder to the thirteen-year-old Eve in me that God always knew to expect something like this out of me.

The day-to-day structure, organization, and creativity of Woman Evolve would not be made possible without our incredible team. Thank you for not just doing the work of getting things done but believing in the work that we're getting done.

I want to give a special thanks to MAC Creative Agency and the Chandy Group for making crazy ideas become wombs of transformation for countless women. Your reward for dealing with me is in heaven.

There's no way this book would be possible without Shaniece Jones acting as security to protect my space and energy so I could tap in. You're not the boss of me, Shaniece, but if I was ever looking for someone to be the boss of me, you would be the first person in line.

My parents and siblings have been in my corner, watching me gradually evolve and shielding me every step of the way. I may have been wounded, but I was not destroyed, and it's because their love was my life support.

I am grateful to my children for allowing me to neglect them for about six weeks while I wrote this book. Thank you for chipping in and doing more so this book can echo throughout the world.

To my husband, my best friend, my king, my lover, and the man who always sees me at my potential—I love you! You promised to create an environment for me to flourish. You have constantly delivered on that promise. Everything I do has the fragrance of you.

God, thank You for Your grace and mercy. It's been following me all the days of my life. Thank You for all that You've allowed me to see. It's truly exceedingly and abundantly above all that I was asking for or even imagining. I'll say what You tell me to say and go wherever You send me. Your glory or nothing at all.

NOTES

1. Courtney Connley, "Uber's Bozoma Saint John Says She Should Have Ignored This Career Advice from a Female Executive," CNBC, October 30, 2017, https://www.cnbc.com/2017/10/30/ubers-bozoma-saint-john -on-the-career-advice-she-should-have-ignored.html.

2. Connley, "Uber's Bozoma Saint John."

3. This quote Bill Gates seems to enjoy using originated with a concept explained by engineer and businessman Frank Gilbreth Sr. in an article published in *Popular Science Monthly* in 1920. "Choose a Lazy Person to Do a Hard Job Because That Person Will Find an Easy Way to Do It," Quote Investigator, February 26, 2014, https://quoteinvestigator.com /2014/02/26/lazy-job/.

4. Astro Teller, "The Unexpected Benefit of Celebrating Failure," filmed February 2016 in Vancouver, BC, TED video, https://www.ted.com /talks/astro_teller_the_unexpected_benefit_of_celebrating_failure.

5. David Grossman, "Secret Google Lab 'Rewards Staff for Failure,'" BBC, January 24, 2014, https://www.bbc.com/news/technology-25880738.

6. Grossman, "Secret Google Lab 'Rewards Staff for Failure.'"

7. Alexa K. Stuifbergen et al., "The Use of Individualized Goal Setting to Facilitate Behavior Change in Women with Multiple Sclerosis," *Journal of Neuroscience Nursing* 35, no. 2 (April 2003): 94–99, 106, https:// search.proquest.com/openview/e77ae438bf007ebeaf5890efccd7929 8/1?pq-origsite=gscholar&cbl=48278; Geoffrey James, "What Goal-Setting Does to Your Brain," *Inc.*, October 23, 2019, https://www .inc.com/geoffrey-james/what-goal-setting-does-to-your-brain-why -its-spectacularly-effective.html.

ABOUT THE AUTHOR

SARAH JAKES ROBERTS is a businesswoman, bestselling author, and media personality who expertly balances career, ministry, and family. She is the founder of Woman Evolve, a multimedia platform dedicated to engaging and empowering the modern woman of faith. She has been the driving force behind grassroots marketing for films, publications, and community programs that inspire and uplift people of all ages and backgrounds.

Sarah is the daughter of Bishop T. D. Jakes and Mrs. Serita Jakes. Alongside her husband, Touré Roberts, she copastors a dynamic community of artists and professionals in Los Angeles, California, and Denver, Colorado. Together they have six beautiful children and reside in Los Angeles.